THE
TOP 100 RECIPES
for BRAINY KIDS

Christine Bailey

GREAT WAYS TO MAXIMIZE YOUR CHILD'S POTENTIAL

DUNCAN BAIRD PUBLISHERS

LONDON

The Top 100 Recipes for Brainy Kids
Christine Bailey

Distributed in the USA and Canada by
Sterling Publishing Co., Inc.
387 Park Avenue South, New York, NY 10016-8810

This edition first published in the UK and USA in 2009 by
Duncan Baird Publishers Ltd
Sixth Floor, Castle House
75–76 Wells Street, London W1T 3QH

Copyright © Duncan Baird Publishers 2009
Text copyright © Christine Bailey 2009
Commissioned photography © Duncan Baird Publishers 2009

Commissioned photography: Simon Smith
Food and prop stylist: Mari Williams

Library of Congress Cataloging-in-Publication Data
Bailey, Christine, 1970-
  The top 100 recipes for brainy kids : great ways to maximize
your child's potential / Christine Bailey.
    p. cm.
  Includes index.
  ISBN 978-1-84483-852-3
  1. Children--Nutrition. 2. Cookery. I. Title. II. Title: Top one
hundred recipes for brainy kids.
  RJ206.B25 2009
  641.5'622--dc22
                                          2009014887

10 9 8 7 6 5 4 3 2 1

Typeset in Helvetica Condensed

I would like to thank everyone at Duncan
Baird Publishers, especially Deirdre and
Nicole, for their ongoing help and advice
with this book. Special thanks to my
wonderful, supportive husband Chris and
three beautiful, healthy children Nathan,
Isaac, and Simeon, who have enjoyed taste
testing all the recipes.

Color reproduction by Colourscan, Singapore
Printed in China by Imago

For information about custom editions, special sales,
or premium and corporate purchases, please contact
Sterling Special Sales Department at 800-805-5489
or specialsales@sterlingpub.com.

Publisher's Note
The information in this book is not intended as a substitute for
professional medical advice and treatment. If you are pregnant
or breastfeeding, or have any special dietary requirements
or medical conditions, it is recommended that you consult a
medical professional before following any of the information
or recipes contained in this book. Duncan Baird Publishers,
or any other persons who have been involved in working on
this publication, cannot accept responsibility for any errors
or omissions, inadvertent or not, that may be found in the
recipes or text, or for any problems that may arise as a result
of preparing one of these recipes or following the advice
contained in this work.

Notes on the Recipes
Unless otherwise stated:
Use large eggs, and medium fruit and vegetables
Use fresh ingredients, including herbs and chilies
1 tsp = 5ml   1 tbsp = 15ml   1 cup = 240ml

Symbols are used to identify even small amounts of an
ingredient. Dairy foods may include cow, goat, or sheep milk.
Check the manufacturer's labeling to ensure cheeses are
vegetarian. Give only the relevantly identified foods to those
children with a food allergy or intolerance.

contents

KEY TO SYMBOLS

V Recipe contains no meat, poultry, game, fish, shellfish, or animal by-products, such as gelatin.

Recipe contains no gluten-based grains or grain products, including wheat, barley, rye, oats, spelt, wheat bran, oat bran, and barley malt syrup.

Recipe contains no wheat, wheat flour, or wheat-based grain products, including wheat pasta or noodles, bulgar, couscous, semolina, wheat bran, wheat germ, and wheat starch.

Recipe contains no cow, sheep, or goat milk, and no cheese, cream, yogurt, butter, or other dairy products.

Recipe contains no egg, either as yolks or whites, or egg-based products.

Recipe contains no nuts, including almonds, peanuts, pine nuts, and walnuts; nut products or nut oils.

Recipe contains no seeds (flax, hemp, pumpkin, sesame, and sunflower) or seed oils, including vegetable oil.

Recipe contains no citrus fruits or zest, including oranges, grapefruit, lemons, limes, clementines, satsumas, and tangerines; or citric-acid preservatives.

Recipe contains no added sugar, including white sugar, brown sugar, molasses, fructose, honey, maple syrup, and brown rice syrup.

Recipe contains no soy or soy-based products, including tofu, tempeh, tamari, soy sauce, miso, and soy milk.

INTRODUCTION

From the moment a child is born, nerve cells or neurons in the brain are making connections by the thousands. They form myriad pathways that build up within the brain to control every function—from breathing, sleeping, speech, and walking to every aspect of learning and behavior. This enormous task of brain development occurs at an incredible rate and, in the first year alone, billions of networks take shape in the brain, guiding these functions to connect with the child's world.

Research being undertaken today shows that giving your child the right kinds of foods with the right balance of nutrients can have a profound and beneficial effect on intellectual development and behavior. With the optimum diet, your child will be able to concentrate well, regulate their behavior, and have a constant supply of energy for clear thinking.

ABOUT THIS BOOK

This book provides clear guidance on which foods to include in your child's diet and features 100 delicious recipes. Each one is packed with nutrients to maximize your children's brain function and help improve their overall mental capacity. Many of the recipes are quick and easy to prepare and can be enjoyed by the whole family. This book is aimed at school-age children, but many of the recipes are also suitable for three- and four- year-olds.

Try to enjoy these recipes as a family and eat together as often as you can—also bear in mind that the number of servings will vary depending upon who's eating. I've calculated average portion sizes only, so make more or less of a dish according to the ages and appetites around the table.

Every recipe provides a guide to its specific brain-boosting ingredients to give you the knowledge to choose meals freely according to your own family's likes and dislikes. Feel free to mix and match the recipes in the book, or simply follow my serving suggestions.

Special diets

Reactions to foods, perhaps as a result of an allergy or intolerance, can result in a variety of symptoms that can be detrimental to learning, including poor concentration, irritability, mood swings, and behavioral problems. If you suspect your child is allergic to certain foods, always consult your doctor or a nutritionist about allergy testing before eliminating any food from his or her diet. Once you have a confirmed diagnosis, use the symbols given at the top of each recipe (see page 6) to choose those that are suitable for your child. I've included recipes free from a variety of common allergens, including wheat, gluten, nuts, seeds, citrus, eggs, and soy; and there are vegetarian and vegan recipes, too. The menu plans on pages 140–143 give ideas for a week's worth of meals for some of these special diets.

CLEVER CARBOHYDRATES

To function optimally, a child's brain needs a constant but even supply of fuel —too little fuel and your child will find it difficult to concentrate, but too much can lead to hyperactivity. The brain's fuel is glucose, which is supplied primarily from the starches and sugars in carbohydrate. However, not all carbohydrate is the same.

Healthy carbohydrate, which provides an even release of fuel and helps balance energy levels, is known as complex carbohydrate. Whole grains, vegetables, fruits, and beans and legumes are all forms of complex carbohydrate because the body takes longer to digest them and they release their sugars at a slower rate.

Refined carbohydrate is not so good. It includes white foods, such as white bread, white pasta, white rice, white-flour products, and sugary, processed foods, such as cakes, cookies, breakfast cereals, and carbonated drinks. Refined carbohydrate is broken down and absorbed by the body quickly, leading to sudden surges in blood glucose (and, therefore, energy) levels, followed by energy slumps. These fluctuations can lead to extreme fatigue, poor concentration, mood swings, irritability, and sudden changes in behavior. If your child often craves pizza, pasta, sugar, and candy, he or she might be suffering from blood-sugar imbalances caused by these foods.

Regulating blood-sugar levels

One of the best ways to monitor the relative value of carbohydrate foods is to use measurements known as the glycemic index (GI) and glycemic load (GL). Foods with a low GI or GL release their sugars at a slower rate. Focus on including these foods in your children's diets to help keep their energy and concentration levels at an optimum throughout the day. Here are my top tips for blood-sugar balance.

• **Combine protein with carbohydrate foods** Eating protein-rich food with carbohydrates slows down the speed at which the body breaks down the sugars and absorbs them into the bloodstream. So, giving your children a handful of nuts with a piece of fruit or spreading peanut butter on whole-grain toast provides good brain balance. Similarly, a little healthy fat (such as monounsaturated fat or essential fats; see pages 11–13) and fiber-rich food (whole grains, vegetables, fruits, beans, and legumes) can help slow down the release of sugars from carbohydrates. Try giving your children morning cereal with plain yogurt and a sprinkling of nuts and seeds; for lunch, top wholewheat crackers with hummus or cheese; for dinner, toss salmon with wholewheat pasta and lots of vegetables.

- **Focus on whole grains** These are complex carbohydrates with low GI and GL scores. They include wholewheat, brown basmati rice, corn, millet, buckwheat, barley, rye, quinoa, oats, and wholewheat pasta and breads.

- **Include plenty of whole foods** The less processed a food is, the lower its GI and GL scores. Avoid prepacked and convenience foods, which contain high amounts of added sugar (see page 18).

- **Make a good start** Sugary cereals and white toast in the morning are a sure way to send blood-sugar levels rocketing. Switch to wholewheat toast with some protein like eggs, beans, or nut butters, or choose an oat-based cereal with a handful of seeds and berries.

- **Switch to healthier sugars** Agave nectar, which is extracted from the Mexican agave plant, is 25 percent sweeter than cane sugar—so you can use much less. It also has a low GI score, making it a great alternative to honey or maple syrup. Xylitol is a natural sugar extracted from the fiber of fruits and vegetables. It has one-third of the calories of cane sugar and a low GI score. Molasses, a concentrated form of cane sugar, is rich in minerals, including iron and calcium, and can be useful when used in moderation.

- **Provide regular meals and snacks** Keep your child's blood sugar levels on an even keel by making sure they eat regularly throughout the day. Be sure your child gets a good breakfast, lunch, and dinner, plus one or two snacks daily, such as nuts, seeds, dips, and vegetable sticks.

BRAINY FATS

The brain is composed of 60 percent fat and uses fat to manufacture its cell membranes and neuron pathways. Like carbohydrate, however, not all fat is equal. For the brain to function optimally, we have to provide foods containing the right types of fat. Among the most important are the essential fats—omega 3 and omega 6—which the body cannot make for itself and must, therefore, get from food. Studies show that a deficiency in essential fats is linked to learning difficulties, attention deficit disorder, dyslexia, depression, memory difficulties, and behavioral problems.

Omega-3 fatty acids

The body needs a good supply of long-chained omega-3 fatty acids known as eicosapentaenoic acid (EPA) and docosahexaenoic acid (DHA) to build brain cells. Flax seeds, walnuts, and pumpkin

EASY WAYS TO BOOST BRAIN FATS

- Grind up a mixture of flax, sunflower, and pumpkin seeds and sprinkle them over whole-grain cereals, stir them into oatmeal or add them to fruit smoothies.
- Instead of using olive oil to make salad dressings, use an Omega 3-6-9 oil (available from health-food stores) or flax-seed oil.
- Add omega-rich oils to smoothies or drizzle them over cooked grains, pasta, vegetables, and soups just before serving.
- Switch to omega-rich eggs and fortified milk and experiment with tofu. Try my Tofu Noodles on page 121 or use diced tofu in place of chicken or turkey in other recipes.
- Incorporate nuts and seeds into toppings for fruit crumbles.

and hemp seeds all contain the "parent" omega-3 fatty acid, alpha linolenic acid (ALA), which the body converts to EPA and DHA. This conversion process can be inefficient, however, so it's better to give your children foods that are already naturally rich in EPA and DHA. Oily fish, such as mackerel, salmon, sardines, and fresh tuna, provide the best source.

Omega-6 fatty acids

The parent omega-6 fat is known as linoleic acid (LA) and it is found in most nuts and seeds. The body converts LA into active gamma-linolenic acid (GLA), which is found naturally in evening primrose oil and borage oil. (A derivative of GLA known as DGLA is found in high concentrations in the brain.)

Children's brains also need another omega-6 fat called arachidonic acid (AA). AA is present in meat and dairy foods, but the body can also produce it using GLA and LA. In this case, because meat and dairy foods tend to be high in saturated (unhealthy) fat, it's better for children to obtain AA from GLA and LA, rather than from foods high in saturated fats.

Omega fats in practice

Studies show that many children are deficient in essential fats, particularly in the omega-3 fats EPA and DHA and the omega-6 fat GLA. To be confident your children are getting enough, try to include oily fish once or twice a week in their diet, plus give them a daily intake of nuts and seeds. (See the box on page 11 for some ideas how to accomplish this.)

While rich in omega 3, certain larger oily fish, such as fresh tuna, can contain toxins such as mercury, so limit each child's consumption to two or three portions a month. Canned tuna is not as high in omega 3 as fresh because the canning process removes some of the fats.

Finally, it's worth noting that omega-3 and omega-6 fats are heat sensitive, so don't be tempted to cook with their oils, and where possible eat nuts and seeds in their raw state.

Additional brain-boosting fats

Another group of important fats is the phospholipids—phosphatidyl choline and phosphatidyl serine. These fats are present in every cell membrane in our body. They are crucial for the production of nerve cells, as well has for helping brain cells to communicate with each other. In addition, the body converts phosphatidyl choline into acetylcholine, an important memory neurotransmitter.

You can find phospholipids in fish, eggs, peanuts, soy, and organ meats, and as a supplement known as lecithin granules. Sensitive to heat, these fats can be destroyed when exposed to high temperatures, so avoid frying eggs, fish, and organ meats, opting for healthier cooking methods such as poaching, boiling, broiler, or baking instead.

PROTEIN POWER

Protein provides the body with its building blocks, known chemically as amino acids. In the brain, the body needs amino acids to make neurotransmitters, the chemical messengers that influence mood, memory, mental performance, and alertness.

There are 23 amino acids altogether, but, like fats, some amino acids are "essential," meaning that our body has to manufacture them from the food we eat. For the body to use amino acids properly, children need all nine essential amino acids in the correct proportions on a regular basis.

Complete and incomplete proteins

Meat, fish, eggs, soy, and dairy products are known as complete proteins because they contain good amounts of all nine of

FOODS FOR SPECIFIC BRAIN FUNCTIONS

NEUROTRANSMITTERS	ROLE IN THE BRAIN	GOOD FOOD SOURCES
Adrenaline, noradrenaline, and dopamine	Mood-boosting, stimulating, motivating; help tackle stress	Foods rich in the amino acids tyrosine and phenylalanine: meat, fish, nuts, seeds, bananas, eggs, oats, avocados, dairy products, and beans
GABA	Calming; helps improve focus, learning, and memory	Fish, especially mackerel; wheat bran; and glutamine-rich foods, such as beef, fish, poultry, eggs, and dairy
Serotonin	Mood-boosting, calming; helps regulate memory and learning	Synthesized from tryptophan-rich foods, especially when combined with carbohydrates: brown rice, cottage cheese, poultry, beans, peanuts, nuts, seeds, baked potatoes, soy
Acetylcholine	Helps improve alertness, memory, learning, focus, and cognitive ability	Made from choline-rich foods: lecithin, eggs, peanuts, brewer's yeast, fish, wheat germ, soybeans, organ meats, wholewheat

the essential amino acids that children need (for adults, there are only eight). Grains, vegetables, legumes, and fruits are incomplete because they contain an inadequate amount of these essential amino acids. To give your child the right balance, you must combine incomplete-protein foods—this is particularly important for vegetarian or vegan children. The key is to offer a variety of protein foods daily.

VITAL VITAMINS AND MINERALS

Vitamins and minerals are crucial for converting glucose into energy, amino acids into neurotransmitters, and essential fats into their active constituents. A table of the most important vitamins and minerals for brain function, and where to find them, appears on page 16, but there is one group of vitamins and several minerals that deserve special mention.

The B Vitamins

These vital nutrients play a key role in producing neurotransmitters and energy for the body's cells. As they are water-soluble, your child will excrete them in his or her urine, so make sure to provide meals rich in B vitamins daily.

Mighty minerals

Calcium and magnesium are great calming minerals and are important for the function of nerve and muscle cells. Zinc is crucial for memory, and boron is important for mental performance, memory, attention, and dexterity.

OTHER NEURON ESSENTIALS

Carbohydrates, essential fats, protein, vitamins, and minerals provide the core nutrients your children's brains need for optimum function. Several other substances in food, however, also have key roles to play in brain health.

Antioxidants

Found in fruit and vegetables, especially those that are brightly colored, antioxidants help protect brain cells against damage by chemically active molecules known as "free radicals." Encourage your children to eat a wide variety of differently colored fruits and vegetables. If you have to, disguise healthy veg by chopping it into pasta sauces, stews, and casseroles, and present fruit by blending it in delicious

THE IQ BOOSTERS

Key vitamins and minerals the brain needs to function effectively, and where to find them.

VITAMIN/MINERAL	KEY FOOD SOURCES	SIGNS OF DEFICIENCY
Vitamin A	Dairy, meat, fish, eggs; fruit and vegetables (as betacarotene)	Poor vision, poor growth
B Vitamins	Whole grains, green leafy vegetables, eggs, meat, fish, seeds, legumes	Low energy, depression, poor memory, anxiety
Vitamin C	Fresh fruits and vegetables	Depression, infections, **low immunity**
Vitamin E	Nuts and seeds and their oils, olives, leafy greens, wheat germ	Digestive problems, tingling in hands and feet, nerve damage
Folic acid	Green leafy vegetables, fortified cereals, beans, legumes	Irritability, mental fatigue, poor memory, insomnia, depression
Calcium	Dairy, green leafy vegetables, dried fruits, soy, canned fish with bones	Anxiety, insomnia, irritability
Iron	Green leafy vegetables, meat, eggs, legumes, molasses, fortified cereals	Low energy, fatigue, poor mental function, depression
Magnesium	Green vegetables, nuts, seeds, beans	Irritability, anxiety, insomnia, hyperactivity, fluctuating energy
Manganese	Whole grains, pineapple, nuts, seeds, beans, green leafy vegetables	Dizziness, fluctuating energy
Zinc	Seafood, fish, nuts, seeds	Lack of concentration, loss of appetite, poor mental function
Vitamin D	Oily fish, fortified milk, sunlight	Mood swings, depression

smoothies— you can even turn smoothies into popsicles if you wish.

Probiotics

Eating healthily is one thing, but your children also need to have a healthy digestive system to optimize how well their young bodies absorb the nutrients from the food you feed them.

One of the simplest ways to promote gut health is to limit, as often as you can, the amount of antibiotics your child receives. Antibiotics can cause an imbalance in the "healthy" bacteria in the gut. They can also weaken the gut membrane and hamper the absorption of nutrients.

There are all sorts of ways to boost the levels of healthy bacteria (probiotics) in the gut. You can give a probiotic supplement, but probiotics also occur naturally in many foods, including plain yogurt, fermented milk, miso, tempeh, sauerkraut, and some soy drinks. Prebiotics, which help stimulate the growth of beneficial bacteria in the gut, are worth stocking up on, too. Good sources include bananas, berries, asparagus, garlic, wheat, oats, barley, Jerusalem artichokes, onions, and endive.

Zinc and glutamine can also promote gut health, so include lean meats, eggs, fish, nuts, and seeds in your child's diet.

The fluid factor

Although water isn't a nutrient, it has a vital part to play in brain health. Dehydration has been shown to contribute to poor concentration and memory, as well as tiredness, headaches, and a host of other health complaints—yet most children don't drink enough water. Even as little as 1 to 2 percent dehydration can affect mental performance.

Water, pure and simple, is by far the best fluid for your child's brain. However, if they are used to sugary-flavored juices or squash, meet them half way at first by diluting pure fruit juice 50:50 with water.

Other good options for increasing fluid intake include milk and pure fruit smoothies—especially if they contain milk or yogurt to help slow down the release of fruit sugar into the bloodstream. For older children and teenagers try herbal or fruit teas and rooibos (redbush) tea.

THE BRAIN DRAINERS

Just as a good diet can enhance brain development, function, and performance, a poor diet can have an adverse affect on the way your child's brain works.

Say no to bad sugars

Refined sugar has little nutritional value and can deplete vitamins and minerals from the body and lead to blood-sugar imbalance. Unfortunately, many processed foods, both sweet and savory, and many children's drinks contain lots of sugar.

Also beware of foods and drinks labeled "sugar free." These are not necessarily better, as they often contain artificial sweeteners, such as aspartame and saccharin, which have been linked with health and behavioral problems.

The recipes in this book will help you keep the number of refined sugars in your child's diet to a minimum. Read labels carefully and, wherever possible, focus on products containing "a little" sugar per 100g (see box, opposite).

READING FOODS LABELS

Follow these general guidelines for "a lot" and "a little" per 100g of food.

	A LOT	A LITTLE
Sugars	10g	2g
Total fat	20g	3g
Saturated fat	5g	1g
Sodium	0.5g	0.1g

Steer clear of harmful fats

Saturated fats, which are found in animal products, such as meat and dairy foods, and fats that have been "damaged" during heating or processing (known as trans and hydrogenated fats) interfere with the conversion of essential fats to DHA and GLA. Avoid them by steering clear of fried and processed foods, including fast foods, ready-to-eat meals, take-outs, margarines, cakes, and cookies. For cooking, use olive oil, coconut oil, and canola oil, which are more heat-stable.

Reduce the chemical load

Pesticides, additives, and preservatives can all adversely affect your child's health and behavior and interfere with the body's ability to harness essential brain nutrients. Opt for organic foods as much as possible, and whenever buying processed foods read the labels closely to determine what additives and colorings they contain.

Protect your children from exposure to heavy metals as much as you can. Keep down their intake of larger fish (see page 12) and avoid using aluminum cookware and foil to cook and store their food.

There's another category of chemicals that children don't need in their lives: stimulants, such as caffeine. We might think of caffeine as an adult vice, found in coffee and tea, but it is also in cola, energy drinks, and chocolate. Caffeine and other stimulants disrupt blood-sugar levels and can lead to erratic behavior. If your child likes a hot drink, switch to caffeine-free alternatives such as rooibos (redbush) tea, herbal teas, or natural coffee substitutes, such as chicory or barley-based drinks.

GETTING STARTED

Incorporating these guidelines and the recipes that follow into your life can help guarantee optimal brain development and mental focus for your growing child.

BREAKFASTS

A decent breakfast is essential for children to perform well at school, concentrate, and feel alert. The nourishment and energy from a healthy breakfast replenish vital brain nutrients and help maintain steady blood-sugar levels—crucial for keeping youngsters energized throughout the morning. That's why this chapter is filled with mouthwatering recipes to tempt even the most reluctant breakfast-eater. From delicious smoothies and quick portable bites to more leisurely dishes for weekend treats, a nutritious breakfast makes a real difference to how your children feel and function. So, kick-start their day with delicious choices such as Date & Walnut Muffins, Zesty Citrus Crêpes, or Vegetable Röstis with Poached Eggs.

001

Ⓥ ✹ ✵ ✺ ◎ ◎ ✹ ◎ ◎ ◉

apricot & tofu boost

This sweet and fruity smoothie is quick and easy to make when time is tight on a busy morning. Protein-packed tofu can help slow down the release of sugars into the bloodstream, so your child can maintain a steady focus all morning long.

SERVES 4

PREPARATION
5 minutes

STORAGE
Best drunk immediately, but it will keep 3 to 4 hours in the refrigerator.

SERVE THIS WITH ...
Giant Baked Beans on Toasted Rye (see page 38) wholewheat toast

HEALTH BENEFITS
Apricots are packed with betacarotene, lycopene, and vitamin C: powerful antioxidants needed to quench free-radical damage to cells and tissues and maintain good eyesight. Dried apricots also have plenty of iron, which is essential for learning.

3 apricots, pitted
3 ready-to-eat dried apricots
1 small peach, pitted

²/₃ cup pineapple juice
9 oz. silken tofu

1 Blend all the ingredients in a blender until smooth and creamy.
2 Divide the drink into four glasses and serve.

Ⓥ Ⓧ Ⓧ Ⓞ Ⓞ Ⓧ Ⓘ Ⓧ

pink zinc heaven

Bursting with antioxidants, fiber, B vitamins, and zinc, this vibrant pink smoothie contains a excellent combination of brain-boosting nutrients. Adding flax-seed oil and tahini is a great way to increase essential fats in your child's diet.

1¼ cups strawberries
heaped 1 cup raspberries
2 passion fruit, flesh strained
1 banana

1 tbsp. tahini
1 tsp. omega-blend oil
  or flax-seed oil
1 cup plain yogurt

1 Blend all the ingredients in a blender until smooth and creamy.
2 Divide the drink into four glasses and serve.

SERVES 4

PREPARATION
5 minutes

STORAGE
Best drunk immediately,
but it will keep 3 to 4 hours
in the refrigerator.

SERVE THIS WITH...
Vegetable Röstis with Poached
  Eggs (see page 34)
wholewheat pita bread

HEALTH BENEFITS
Sesame seeds (from the tahini),
yogurt, and berries are all
rich sources of brain-boosting
zinc, which improves memory
and cognitive skills and
encourages growth and
development.

Ⓥ ⓧ ⓧ Ⓞ Ⓞ ⓧ Ⓞ Ⓞ ⓧ

peach & raspberry shake

SERVES 4

PREPARATION
5 minutes

STORAGE
Best drunk immediately,
but it will keep 3 to 4 hours
in the refrigerator.

SERVE THIS WITH...
Breakfast Bars (see page 32)
Oaty Pancakes with
 Hot-Smoked Salmon
 (see page 37)

HEALTH BENEFITS
Peaches are a rich source
of protective vitamin C and
phytochemicals, as well as iron,
which helps to prevent anemia
and maintain energy levels.
Combined with protein from the
milk and yogurt, they provide
amino acids, such as tyrosine,
which help to increase alertness
and concentration.

Your children will love this fabulous breakfast
shake. The mixed seeds and fruit provide the
essential fatty acids they'll need to keep going
and maintain their concentration all morning.

2 peaches, pitted
¼ cup mixed seeds, such as
 sunflower, sesame, and
 pumpkin

1¼ cups raspberries
2 tsp. flax-seed oil
¾ cup plain yogurt
⅓ cup milk

1 Blend all the ingredients together in a blender until
smooth and creamy.
2 Divide the drink into four glasses and serve.

Ⓥ Ⓧ Ⓧ Ⓞ Ⓞ Ⓧ Ⓞ Ⓞ Ⓧ

blueberry brain-booster milkshake

Sweet and delicious, this is one of the healthiest smoothies you can make to boost your child's performance. The almonds give it a wonderfully rich, creamy texture.

¼ cup almonds, soaked in
   water overnight, then
   drained

1¾ cups blueberries
1 small banana
²/₃ cup milk

1 Blend all the ingredients in a blender until smooth and creamy.
2 Divide the drink into four glasses and serve immediately.

SERVES 4

PREPARATION
5 minutes

STORAGE
Best drunk immediately.

SERVE THIS WITH...
Popeye Baked Eggs
  (see page 33)
rye bread toast

HEALTH BENEFITS
Almonds are rich in calcium and magnesium for nerve and muscle functions, and in vitamin E to protect cells from free-radical damage. Nuts and milk are valuable sources of protein and also help to balance the absorption of natural fruit sugars and avoid those midmorning energy slumps that ruin concentration.

005

brain-berry muesli

HEALTH BENEFITS
Blueberries are a superfood for the brain, one of the best sources of antioxidant phytonutrients, which support healthy brain function and improve cognitive abilities. Almonds contain memory-boosting B vitamins and zinc, plus protein to help the brain function.

A crunchy muesli that's not loaded with sugar and saturated fat, this is bound to be a favorite with your children. Toasting the oats and nuts creates a wonderful flavor, and the seeds provide essential nutrients for brain health.

2 cups rolled oats
¼ cup unsweetened coconut
flakes
4 tbsp. roughly chopped
macadamia nuts
¼ cup ground almonds
¼ cup pumpkin seeds
¼ cup sunflower seeds
1 tsp. cinnamon

½ cup mixed dried berries,
such as cranberries,
blueberries, and cherries
milk, to serve

Berry Compote:
1 cup mixed berries, fresh
or frozen
3 tbsp. apple juice

SERVES 4

PREPARATION + COOKING
10 + 10 minutes

STORAGE
The muesli will keep in an
airtight container up to
2 weeks. The compote will keep
in the refrigerator up to 2 days.

SERVE THIS WITH...
Giant Baked Beans on Toasted
Rye (see page 38)

1 Put the rolled oats, coconut, and macadamia nuts
in a nonstick skillet and cook over low heat, stirring
frequently, 2 to 3 minutes until light brown. Remove
from the heat and leave to cool.

2 Put the oat mixture in a bowl and stir in the almonds,
pumpkin and sunflower seeds, cinnamon, and berries.

3 To make the berry compote, put the berries in a pan
with the apple juice. Heat slowly until just boiling, then
simmer 7 minutes, or until the berries are soft; set aside
to cool.

4 Spoon the muesli into four bowls and add milk to taste.
Serve topped with the berry compote.

If your child is
intolerant or
allergic to dairy,
use soy or rice
milk instead of
cow's milk.

Ⓥ ⓧ ⓧ Ⓞ Ⓞ ⓧ

millet & apple cereal

Millet makes a creamy, gluten-free cereal that's a good alternative to oatmeal. It is combined here with apples, apricots, nuts, and seeds to provide a brain-boosting breakfast.

SERVES 4

PREPARATION + COOKING
10 + 35 minutes

STORAGE
Leftovers will keep in the refrigerator up to 2 days.

SERVE THIS WITH
Pink Zinc Heaven (see page 23)

HEALTH BENEFITS
Millet is rich in magnesium, which is well known for its calming properties. It is also essential for the functioning of more than 300 different enzymes in the body, including those responsible for stabilizing blood-sugar levels and producing neurotransmitters.

¾ cup millet
2 small eating apples, peeled, cored, and diced
²/₃ cup milk
¹/₃ cup cashew nuts

4 ready-to-eat dried apricots
1 tsp. cinnamon
1 tbsp. honey or agave nectar
1 tbsp. ground flax seeds

1 Put the millet in a saucepan, pour in 3 cups water, and bring to a boil, stirring. Reduce the heat, cover the pan, and simmer 15 minutes.

2 Stir in the apples and continue simmering 15 minutes longer until almost all the water is absorbed. Remove from the heat and set aside.

3 Blend the milk, nuts, apricots, cinnamon, honey, and flax seeds in a blender or food processor until smooth.

4 Stir the nut mixture into the millet and serve hot or cold.

fruit & seed granola

This crunchy yet chewy breakfast cereal is far healthier than store-bought versions. The nuts and seeds provide plenty of protein and essential fats, which, together with the slow-release energy from the oats, help your child to stay focused all morning.

2¾ cups rolled oats
½ cup slivered almonds
½ cup roughly chopped pecans
½ cup sunflower seeds
½ cup pumpkin seeds
4 tbsp. sesame seeds

3 tbsp. light olive or canola oil
scant 1 cup apple juice
½ cup roughly chopped
   ready-to-eat dried apricots
heaped ½ cup dried mixed
   berries or cherries

1 Preheat the oven to 350°F.
2 Put the rolled oats, nuts, and seeds into a large bowl. Mix the oil with the apple juice and stir it into the dry ingredients.
3 Spread out the mixture on a large baking sheet and bake 30 minutes, or until golden, stirring halfway through cooking. Stir in the dried apricots and berries and bake 5 minutes longer.
4 Leave to cool before serving or storing.

SERVES 4 TO 6

PREPARATION + COOKING
10 + 35 minutes

STORAGE
Store in an airtight container up to 2 weeks.

SERVE THIS WITH...
Popeye Baked Eggs
  (see page 33)
glass of freshly squeezed
  orange juice

HEALTH BENEFITS
Pecans contain choline to aid memory and brain development. Almonds provide phenylalanine: important for the production of mood-boosting neurotransmitters, such as dopamine, noradrenaline, and adrenaline.

Ⓥ ⊗ ⊗ ◯ ◯ ⊗

tropical yogurt pots

This easy-to-assemble, crunchy fruit mix is based on the popular store-bought versions that are often loaded with sugar and drain your child of energy. You can prepare and assemble these the night before—which makes them ideal when you're running late in the morning.

SERVES 4

PREPARATION + COOKING
10 + 2 minutes

STORAGE
Prepare in advance and store in the refrigerator up to 1 day. Store the nut-and-seed topping in an airtight container up to 2 days.

SERVE THIS WITH ...
Vegetable Röstis with Poached Eggs (see page 34)
fresh fruit

HEALTH BENEFITS
Tropical fruits, such as persimmon and passion fruit, are rich in the antioxidants vitamin C and betacarotene, which are needed to protect against cell damage. They improve the body's absorption of iron from vegetarian sources.

¼ cup shredded coconut
¼ cup macadamia nuts
3 tbsp. cashew nuts
3 tbsp. pumpkin seeds
1 tbsp. ground flax seeds

4 persimmon, halved
juice of 1 orange
1 cup plain yogurt
2 passion fruit, pulp strained

1 Lightly toast the shredded coconut and nuts in a nonstick skillet 1 to 2 minutes until they are golden brown, stirring frequently.

2 Place the coconut and nuts in a blender with the pumpkin seeds and pulse the power to chop the mixture finely. Transfer to a bowl and stir in the flax seeds.

3 Put the persimmon, orange juice, and yogurt in the blender and blend until smooth.

4 Divide the yogurt mixture into four glasses or bowls and swirl in the passionfruit pulp. Top with the nut and seed mixture and serve.

date & walnut muffins

These delightful muffins are bursting with essential fats, vitamins, and minerals. Dates and bananas are energizing foods and, combined with wholewheat flour, help to provide a steady release of energy.

2¼ cups wholewheat flour
2 tsp. baking powder
1 tsp. baking soda
¼ cup sugar
heaped ¾ cup walnuts, chopped

¾ cup chopped dates
2 large ripe bananas
1¼ cups plain yogurt
5 tbsp. light olive oil
1 egg, beaten

1 Preheat the oven to 350°F and line a 12-hole muffin pan with muffin cases.
2 Mix the flour, baking powder, baking soda, sugar, walnuts, and dates in a large bowl.
3 Mash the bananas in a separate bowl, then stir in the yogurt, oil, and egg. Make a well in the middle of the dry ingredients, pour in the yogurt mixture, and fold both mixtures together until just combined.
4 Spoon the batter into the muffin cases. Bake 20 to 25 minutes until well risen, golden brown, set, and springy to the touch. Leave to cool slightly before serving.

MAKES 12

PREPARATION + COOKING
5 + 25 minutes

STORAGE
Store in an airtight container in the refrigerator up to 3 days or in the freezer up to 3 months.

SERVE THIS WITH...
Pink Zinc Heaven (see page 23)
fresh fruit

HEALTH BENEFITS
Walnuts have long been regarded as a "brain food," not only because of their brainlike appearance, but also owing to their high concentration of omega-3 fats.

010

Ⓥ ⊘ ◐ ◔ ◑ ✖

breakfast bars

MAKES 12 TO 16 BARS

PREPARATION + COOKING
15 + 30 minutes

STORAGE
Store in an airtight container
in the refrigerator up to 3 days
or freeze up to 3 months.

SERVE THIS WITH...
Blueberry Brain-Booster
  Milkshake (see page 25)
fresh fruit

HEALTH BENEFITS
Peanut butter is rich in
monounsaturated fat,
antioxidants, and a wealth of
vitamins and minerals, including
folic acid and niacin. Peanuts
provide plenty of protein for
growth and development.

For a delicious, protein-packed breakfast
on the run, these filling bars are perfect.

olive oil, for greasing
3 cups chopped pitted dates
scant 1 cup apple juice
½ cup peanut butter
2 cups rolled oats

1 cup + 2 tbsp. wholewheat
  flour
2 tbsp. ground flax seeds
1 tsp. baking powder
1 tsp. cinnamon

1 Preheat the oven to 375°F and grease a shallow
10- x 8-inch baking pan with oil.
2 Put the dates and juice in a saucepan and bring to
a boil, then reduce the heat and simmer 1 to 2 minutes.
Cool slightly, then puree in a food processor or blender.
Put just over half the puree in a bowl and set aside.
3 Add the peanut butter to the remaining puree in the
food processor and process again to form a thick paste.
4 Mix the rolled oats, flour, flax seeds, baking powder, and
cinnamon in a bowl. Stir in the peanut butter mixture to form
a sticky dough. Press half the dough into the pan and spread
the date puree on top. Scatter with lumps of the remaining
dough and press by hand to cover the date layer completely.
5 Bake 20 to 25minutes until golden brown. Cool in the pan
10 to 15 minutes before turning out. Cut into small bars
and place on a rack to cool completely, then serve.

Ⓥ Ⓧ Ⓧ Ⓧ Ⓧ Ⓧ Ⓧ Ⓧ Ⓧ

Popeye baked eggs

Creamy spinach and cheese-topped eggs make a comforting, nutritious dish that is simple and speedy to put together.

1 tbsp. butter, plus extra
   for greasing
1½ bags (10-oz.) baby spinach
   leaves, washed
4 eggs

¾ cup crème fraîche
²/₃ cup grated cheddar cheese
freshly ground black pepper
freshly grated nutmeg

1 Preheat the oven to 400°F and grease four individual shallow baking dishes with butter.

2 Melt the butter in a saucepan over low heat and add the spinach. Cover and cook 20 seconds, or until it wilts. Divide the spinach into the prepared dishes and season with a little black pepper.

3 Make a slight indentation in the middle of each portion of spinach and crack 1 egg into each. Carefully spoon the crème fraîche around the eggs. Season with a little nutmeg and sprinkle the grated cheddar over the eggs.

4 Bake 10 to 12 minutes until the eggs are just set. Serve immediately.

SERVES 4

PREPARATION + COOKING
5 + 15 minutes

STORAGE
Best eaten immediately. The cheddar cheese can be grated the night before and stored in an airtight container in the refrigerator.

SERVE THIS WITH ...
wholewheat bread or toast

HEALTH BENEFITS
Spinach is well known for its iron content and for boosting energy and concentration. It is also packed with other key brain nutrients, including vitamins A and B, folic acid, and the calming minerals calcium and magnesium.

012

HEALTH BENEFITS
When it comes to brain food, eggs are nutritional powerhouses, packed with protein, B vitamins, selenium, iodine, vitamin D, and iron. They are also rich in the nutrient choline, a key component of brain-cell membranes, which is used to produce the neurotransmitter acetylcholine, involved with memory.

vegetable röstis with poached eggs

These crisp, golden röstis are a sneaky way to encourage your children to eat more vegetables. Combined with goat cheese and topped with poached eggs, they provide perfect brain fuel.

olive oil, for greasing
1½ cups grated sweet potatoes
¾ cup grated parsnips
6 eggs

2 scallions, chopped
2¾ oz. goat cheese, crumbled
freshly ground black pepper

1 Preheat the oven to 400°F and grease a large baking sheet with oil. Mix the sweet potatoes and parsnips in a bowl and season with pepper.

2 Put 2 of the eggs in a blender or food processor. Add the scallions and cheese and blend until smooth. Pour the mixture into the grated vegetables and mix well.

3 Using a spoon, shape the mixture into 8 equal patties and put them on the baking sheet. Bake 30 to 35 minutes until the patties are golden brown and crisp.

4 Meanwhile, bring a large pan of water to a boil. Break 1 egg into a cup and then gently slide it into the water. Repeat with the remaining eggs and poach 3 to 4 minutes until cooked to taste. Using a slotted spoon, remove the eggs from the pan and drain on paper towels.

5 Put the röstis on plates and top with the eggs. Serve immediately.

SERVES 4

PREPARATION + COOKING
15 + 35 minutes

STORAGE
Make the röstis in advance and reheat in a warm oven while poaching the eggs. Leftovers will keep in the refrigerator up to 1 day.

SERVE THIS WITH ...
Giant Baked Beans
  (see page 38)
fresh fruit

Try experimenting with different cheeses, such as feta or grated cheddar or Gruyère.

Ⓥ ✖ ✖

zesty citrus crêpes

With a sweet, creamy citrus sauce, these crêpes will be a big hit with all the family.

MAKES 6 TO 8 CREPES

PREPARATION + COOKING
10 + 20 minutes

STORAGE
Leftovers will keep in the refrigerator up to 2 days.

SERVE THIS WITH
Pink Zinc Heaven
  (see page 23)
fresh fruit

HEALTH BENEFITS
Oranges are a source of protective vitamin C, which positively affects a child's brain functions.

½ cup + 1 tbsp. all-purpose
  flour
¼ cup wholewheat flour
¼ cup ground flax seeds
grated zest of 1 orange
2 eggs, beaten
1 cup milk
2 tbsp. olive oil

1 orange, peeled and segmented

Creamy Citrus Sauce:
juice and grated zest of
  4 oranges
2 tbsp. honey or agave nectar
1 cup + 2 tbsp. mascarpone
  cheese

1 Sift the flours into a bowl. Stir in the flax seeds and orange zest, then make a well in the middle and add the eggs. Whisk in the milk until a smooth batter forms.
2 Heat a little of the oil in a skillet. Add 2 to 3 tablespoons of batter, tilting the pan to form a crêpe. Cook 1 minute, or until set and brown underneath, then flip the crêpe and cook the other side 10 to 20 seconds; transfer to a warm plate. Repeat with the remaining batter.
3 To make the sauce, simmer the orange juice, zest, and honey 2 minutes, or until slightly thicker. Put the mascarpone in a bowl and whisk in the orange mixture.
4 Top the crêpes with the sauce and orange segments and serve immediately.

oaty pancakes with hot-smoked salmon

These pancakes are a real treat. Topped with a creamy smoked salmon mixture, they'll give your children a healthy start to the day.

heaped ½ cup rolled oats
²/₃ cup all-purpose flour
1 tsp. baking powder
1 egg, beaten
½ cup milk

1 tbsp. olive oil
7 oz. hot-smoked salmon
5 tbsp. crème fraîche
1 tbsp. chopped dill
grated zest of 1 lemon

1 Put the rolled oats in a food processor and pulse several times to break down the grains. Add the flour and baking powder and pulse to mix lightly. Add the egg. With the processor running, gradually pour in the milk to make a smooth, thick batter.

2 Heat the oil in a skillet. Drop 4 spoonfuls of batter into the skillet to make small pancakes, spacing them apart. Cook 3 minutes, or until just set on top and golden underneath, then turn and cook the other side 1 to 2 minutes until brown underneath. Repeat with the remaining the batter.

3 Flake the salmon into a bowl. Mix in the crème fraîche, dill, and lemon zest. Top the pancakes with the salmon mixture and serve.

MAKES 12 PANCAKES

PREPARATION + COOKING
10 + 15 minutes

STORAGE
Leftovers will keep in the refrigerator up to 2 days.

SERVE THIS WITH …
broiled tomatoes
Blueberry Brain-Booster
  Milkshake (see page 25)

HEALTH BENEFITS
Rolled oats contain beta-glucan, a rich source of soluble fiber, plus magnesium, which helps to stabilize blood-sugar levels and avoid midmorning energy dips. Rolled oats help keep the body fueled for longer.

Ⓥ ⊘ ❶ ✗ ⊘ ⊘ ❶ ✗

giant baked beans on toasted rye

This is a tastier, healthier alternative to sugary canned baked beans, made using soft and creamy lima beans. It is a protein-rich and energizing breakfast.

SERVES 4

PREPARATION + COOKING
5 + 10 minutes

STORAGE
Leftovers will keep in the refrigerator up to 2 days.

SERVE THIS WITH...
good-quality organic sausages
broiled mushrooms

HEALTH BENEFITS
Lima beans are an excellent source of molybdenum, a trace mineral needed for detoxifying sulfites, which are commonly used as a food preservative. A sensitivity to sulfites has been linked to poor concentration, disorientation, and headaches. Lima beans also contain iron, zinc and B vitamins.

1 tbsp. olive oil
1 small red onion, chopped
2 cans (15-oz.) canned lima
    or butter beans, drained
    and rinsed
1 can (15-oz.) crushed
    tomatoes
3 tbsp. tomato paste

pinch of ground allspice
pinch of cinnamon
3 tbsp. apple juice
1 tbsp. tamari
2 tsp. apple cider vinegar
4 slices of rye bread
1 tbsp. chopped parsley

1 Heat the oil in a saucepan. Add the onion and cook 2 to 3 minutes until soft.

2 Stir in the lima beans, tomatoes, tomato paste, spices, apple juice, tamari, and vinegar. Bring to a boil, reduce the heat, and simmer 5 minutes, or until heated through and slightly thicker.

3 Lightly toast the rye bread. Spoon the beans onto the toast and sprinkle with the parsley. Serve immediately.

Ⓥ ⊗ ⊗ ⊗ ⊚ ⊗ ⊗

broiled peaches with macadamia cream

This is a light, fruity breakfast treat that is rich in protein and essential minerals. The macadamia cream is equally delicious spooned over muesli, cereals, and puddings.

olive oil, for greasing
4 peaches, halved and pitted
3 tbsp. honey or agave nectar
2 tsp. dairy-free margarine

scant 1 cup macadamia nuts
juice of 2 oranges
1 to 2 drops vanilla extract

1 Preheat the oven to 350°F and grease a baking dish with oil. Put the peaches, cut-side up, in the dish, drizzle half the agave nectar over, and dot with the margarine. Bake 10 to 15 minutes until slightly soft.
2 Blend the remaining agave and remaining ingredients in a blender until smooth. Serve the peaches warm with the macadamia cream.

SERVES 4

PREPARATION + COOKING
10 + 15 minutes

STORAGE
The cream will keep in the refrigerator up to 3 days. The cooked peaches will keep in the refrigerator up to 1 day.

SERVE THIS WITH...
Giant Baked Beans on
  Toasted Rye (see page 38)

HEALTH BENEFITS
A good source of fiber, peaches can help to slow down the release of glucose into the bloodstream, helping to maintain energy levels and concentration. They are also rich in protective antioxidants, including vitamin C and betacarotene.

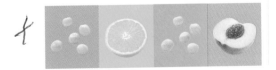

LUNCHES

A nutrient-rich lunch nourishes and energizes children to help them concentrate in the afternoon. The range of recipes in this chapter includes delicious soups, sandwiches, wraps, salads, and temptingly easy hot dishes to suit all occasions. From light meals at home to lunch-box fillers for taking to school or enjoying at weekends, take your pick from this irresistible selection. Try Turkey Noodle Soup, Creamy Salmon & Alfalfa Pitas, Chicken Spring Rolls, or Moroccan Turkey Wraps. A tasty salad enlivens any lunch break, so why not try Cranberry & Almond Quinoa or Thai Chicken Salad? And children are sure to love hot dishes, such as Tuna Kebabs with Pineapple, Pork & Egg-Fried Rice, or delicious Baked Stuffed Peppers.

017

Ⓥ Ⓧ Ⓧ Ⓧ Ⓠ Ⓠ Ⓠ Ⓧ Ⓧ

beet cream soup

This soup's vibrant color is sure to catch your children's attention, and they'll love its smooth, velvety texture, too.

SERVES 4

PREPARATION + COOKING
15 + 55 minutes

STORAGE
Leftovers will keep in the refrigerator up to 1 day or in the freezer up to 1 month.

SERVE THIS WITH...
Seeded Rye Bread
(see page 74)
Fruit Layer Crisp (see page 134)

HEALTH BENEFITS
Beets are full of blood-building folate and protective antioxidants to support neurotransmitter production.

1lb. 2 oz. raw beets, scrubbed
1 tbsp. olive oil
1 onion, chopped
2 garlic cloves, chopped
2 celery stalks, chopped
3 carrots, chopped

3 cups vegetable stock
7 oz. creamed coconut, chopped
2 tsp. apple cider vinegar
freshly ground black pepper
4 tsp. pumpkin seeds, to serve

1 Put the beets in a large saucepan. Cover with boiling water and bring back to a boil, then reduce the heat, cover, and simmer 30 to 40 minutes until tender. Drain the beets, then rub off the skins, holding them under cold water to avoid burning your fingers; chop when cool.

2 Heat the oil in the rinsed-out pan. Add the onion, garlic, celery, and carrots and cook 1 to 2 minutes. Stir in the stock and coconut. Bring to a boil, then reduce the heat and simmer 10 minutes, or until the vegetables are tender. Add the beets.

3 Puree the soup in a blender, then return it to the pan. Add the vinegar. Reheat slowly 2 to 3 minutes and add pepper to taste. Serve sprinkled with the pumpkin seeds.

turkey noodle soup

This speedy soup is rich in protein and also contains plenty of antioxidant-rich vegetables.

5 oz. wholewheat noodles
3 cups turkey or chicken stock
½-in. piece ginger root, peeled and grated
1 garlic clove, crushed
1 tsp. soft brown sugar
1 envelope instant miso soup
pinch of five-spice powder
2 tbsp. tamari

3½ oz. bean sprouts
¾ cup sliced shiitake mushrooms
²/₃ cup trimmed and sliced snow peas
1 cup canned corn kernels, drained
9 oz. roast turkey, shredded
2 tbsp. chopped cilantro leaves

1 Cook the noodles according to the package directions; drain and set aside.

2 Pour the stock into a large saucepan. Add the ginger, garlic, sugar, instant miso soup, five-spice powder, and tamari. Bring to a boil, then reduce the heat and simmer 2 minutes.

3 Add the bean sprouts, mushrooms, snow peas, corn, and turkey and simmer 5 minutes longer.

4 Divide the noodles into four bowls. Ladle the soup over, sprinkle with the cilantro leaves, and serve.

SERVES 4

PREPARATION + COOKING
15 + 15 minutes

STORAGE
Leftovers will keep in the refrigerator up to 1 day.

SERVE THIS WITH...
fresh fruit
Chocolate & Cranberry Brownies (see page 84)

HEALTH BENEFITS
Shiitake mushrooms are rich in iron and antioxidants, which are important nutrients for optimal brain development.

019

Ⓥ ⓧ ⓧ ⓧ ⓧ Ⓞ ⓧ ⓧ Ⓞ Ⓞ ⓧ

tomato & chickpea soup

The chickpeas in this soup create a twist on an old favorite and make a fabulous, healthy lunch that children will devour.

SERVES 4

PREPARATION + COOKING
10 + 20 minutes

STORAGE
Leftovers will keep in the refrigerator up to 2 days or in the freezer up to 3 months.

SERVE THIS WITH
Pumpkin Biscuits (see page 73)
Fruit Gels (see page 136)

HEALTH BENEFITS
Chickpeas are a good source of protein and fiber, which are useful for stabilizing blood-sugar levels. Their iron content helps to boost energy levels and concentration, and they also provide manganese: important for its interaction with a number of enzymes that are essential for energy production and antioxidant defences.

1 tbsp.olive oil
1 red onion, chopped
1 garlic clove, crushed
pinch of cayenne pepper
pinch of ground allspice
¼ tsp. ground cumin
1 can (15-oz.) chickpeas, drained and rinsed

1½ cups strained pureed tomatoes
1 cup vegetable stock
4 sun-dried tomatoes in oil, drained and finely chopped
1 tbsp. chopped parsley
freshly ground black pepper

1 Heat the oil in a saucepan. Add the onion and garlic and cook 2 to 3 minutes. Stir in the cayenne, allspice, and cumin and cook slowly 3 minutes longer, or until the onion is soft.

2 Stir in the chickpeas, tomatoes, stock, and sun-dried tomatoes. Bring to a boil, then reduce the heat and simmer 10 minutes, or until the soup thickens slightly.

3 Season the soup to taste with black pepper, stir in the parsley, and serve.

ⓥ ⓞ ⓧ ⓞ ⓞ ⓧ

veg & pesto panini

Toasted panini make great lunch treats and are an excellent way to slip extra vegetables and nutrient-rich seeds into your child's diet.

1 red bell pepper, seeded and quartered
1 yellow bell pepper, seeded and quartered
1 zucchini, sliced
2 tbsp. olive oil
2 thyme sprigs
6 cherry tomatoes, halved
4 panini, cut in half horizontally

Pesto:
1 garlic clove, chopped
1 oz. basil leaves
2 tbsp. pumpkin seeds
5 tbsp. omega oil or flax-seed oil
1 tbsp. grated Parmesan cheese

1 Preheat the oven to 425°F.

2 In a roasting pan, mix the peppers and zucchini with the olive oil and thyme. Roast 30 minutes, or until tender. Add the tomatoes and roast 10 minutes longer.

3 To make the pesto, put the garlic, basil, and pumpkin seeds in a food processor. Process to form a coarse paste, then add the oil with the motor running to create a smooth pesto. Stir in the cheese.

4 Preheat a sandwich toaster or the boiler. Spread the pesto on the panini halves. Divide the vegetables onto the panini bottoms and replace the tops, pesto-side down, pressing down firmly. Broil 2 to 3 minutes until warm, then serve immediately.

SERVES 4

PREPARATION + COOKING
15 + 50 minutes

STORAGE
Prepare the vegetables in advance and chill them until required; leftovers will keep in the refrigerator up to 1 day. The pesto can be stored in the refrigerator up to 1 week.

SERVE THIS WITH...
fresh fruit salad
Apricot Muesli Bars
  (page 85)

HEALTH BENEFITS
Parmesan cheese is an excellent source of calcium and protein that is rich in amino acids, including tyrosine. It is great for supporting mental alertness and helping the body to cope with everyday stress. Vegetarian versions are available (check labels for information).

Ⓥ ⊗ ⊗ ⊗ ⊗ ⊗ ⊗ ⊗ ⊗ ⊗

*Mexican bean tacos

HEALTH BENEFITS
This recipe combines protein-rich beans, avocado, and grain to provide a full range of amino acids, which are essential for the formation of neurotransmitters, the brain's chemical messengers.

Here's a great weekend lunch that children will love helping to prepare. Easy to assemble, tacos are a fantastic alternative to sandwiches, and are full of energizing nutrients, including B vitamins, calcium, magnesium, and zinc.

2 tbsp. olive oil
1 red onion, chopped
1 garlic clove, crushed
1 small zucchini, diced
1 tsp. Cajun spices
1 can (15-oz.) kidney beans or
  mixed beans, drained
  and rinsed

3 tomatoes, seeded
  and diced
8 x 100% corn taco shells
1 avocado, diced
2 tbsp. chopped cilantro leaves
scant 1 cup grated cheddar
  cheese, grated

SERVES 4

PREPARATION + COOKING
15 + 7 minutes

STORAGE
You can prepare the bean
mixture in advance, then warm
through and add the avocado
immediately before serving.

SERVE THIS WITH...
fresh fruit
Flax-Seed Gingerbread Men
  (see page 78)

1 Heat the oil in a skillet. Add the onion, garlic, zucchini,
and Cajun spices and fry 3 to 4 minutes until the onion
is soft.
2 Stir in the beans and tomatoes and slowly cook
3 minutes longer.
3 Warm the taco shells according to the package directions.
4 Stir the avocado and cilantro into the bean mixture, then
spoon it into the taco shells, top with the grated cheese,
and serve.

Full of healthy
fats, avocado
starts to turn
brown once cut,
so prepare it just
before serving.

Ⓥ Ⓧ Ⓧ Ⓧ Ⓧ Ⓧ Ⓧ Ⓧ Ⓧ

fabulous frittata

This Mediterranean-inspired frittata is packed with antioxidants, brain-boosting fats, and plenty of protein from the eggs and cheese.

SERVES 4–6

PREPARATION + COOKING
5 + 10 minutes

STORAGE
Leftovers will keep in the refrigerator up to 1 day.

SERVE THIS WITH...
carrot sticks
wholewheat toast
Blueberry Muffins
  (see page 87)

HEALTH BENEFITS
Rich in the antioxidant vitamin E and monounsaturated fats, olives and their oil help to prevent free-radical attack and also provide healthy brain fats.

6 eggs
2 tbsp. olive oil
½ cup drained and sliced
   chargrilled baby artichokes
   in oil
8 pitted black olives, halved

1 bottled roasted red bell
   pepper, drained and sliced
2½ oz. goat cheese, crumbled
2 tbsp. chopped basil leaves
freshly ground black pepper

1 Beat the eggs and season with a little black pepper.
2 Heat the oil in a flameproof skillet and add the artichokes, olives, and red pepper. Stir 1 minute, or until heated through. Pour in the eggs and cook 5 to 6 minutes until they are almost set.
3 Preheat the broiler to high. Scatter the goat cheese and basil over the frittata and place the pan under the broiler 2 to 3 minutes until golden. Cut into wedges and serve, or leave to cool before cutting.

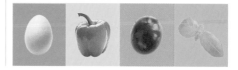

creamy salmon & alfalfa pitas

Forget dull, soggy sandwiches and perk up the brain with these pitas, which are filled with plenty of protein, omega-3 essential fats, and brilliant flavors.

6 small gherkins, finely chopped
¾ cup crème fraîche
2 tbsp. chopped parsley
2 tbsp. chopped dill
2 tsp. lemon juice
1 can (7-oz.) skinless, boneless salmon, drained

4 wholewheat pita breads, halved crosswise
large handful of alfalfa sprouts
freshly ground black pepper

1 Mix the gherkins, crème fraîche, parsley, dill, and lemon juice in a bowl and season with black pepper to taste.
2 Flake the salmon into the herb mixture and mix well.
3 Spoon the salmon mixture into the pita bread halves, top with alfalfa sprouts, and serve.

SERVES 4

PREPARATION
10 minutes

STORAGE
The filling can be made in advance and stored in the refrigerator 2 days.

SERVE THIS WITH...
carrot and celery sticks
cucumber sticks
Banana & Mango Cake
(see page 88)

HEALTH BENEFITS
Alfalfa is packed with enzymes and easily digestible nutrients that are essential for brain health, including B vitamins, folic acid, zinc, calcium, and magnesium. It is also rich in chlorophyll, a powerful blood-builder, and amino acids.

024

SERVES 4

PREPARATION + COOKING
20 + 17 minutes + proving

STORAGE
Leftovers will keep in the refrigerator up to 1 day.

SERVE THIS WITH...
cherry tomatoes
cucumber sticks
red bell-pepper sticks
Fruit Gels (see page 136)

HEALTH BENEFITS
While canned tuna is not as rich in omega-3 essential fats as fresh fish, it does contain some and is an excellent source of high-quality, energizing protein, plus a variety of other important nutrients, including selenium, magnesium, and B vitamins.

tuna & cheese calzone

A delicious Italian-style pasty, this iron- and protein-rich calzone boosts energy levels.

1 cup white bread flour
¾ cup + 1 tbsp. wholewheat
    bread flour
scant 1 tsp. fast-acting
    dry yeast
½ cup warm milk
1 tbsp. olive oil

Filling:
6 oz. baby spinach leaves
1 cup ricotta cheese
1 can (7-oz.) tuna in oil or
    spring water, drained
pinch of freshly grated nutmeg
freshly ground black pepper

1 Put the flours in a bowl with the yeast. Add the milk and oil and mix to form a dough.

2 Knead 10 minutes. Put in a clean bowl, cover, and leave to rise 1 hour, or until double in size.

3 Preheat the oven to 400°F. Put the spinach in a pan with 1 tbsp. water and cook 2 minutes, or until it wilts. Drain well, then put in a bowl with the rest of the filling ingredients.

4 Punch down the dough and divide it into 4 pieces. Roll each piece into a 6¼-inch circle. Put a quarter of the mixture on half of each circle, brush the edges with water, and fold over to enclose. Pinch the dough together to seal. Brush the tops with oil.

5 Bake 10 to 15 minutes until golden, then serve.

griddled chicken & guacamole rolls

This nutritious lunch will satisfy hunger pangs.

3 skinless, boneless chicken
   breast halves
3 tbsp. olive oil
1 garlic clove, crushed
½ tsp. jerk seasoning
4 wholewheat rolls, halved
2 tbsp. sour cream

Guacamole:
1 avocado
½ red onion, finely chopped
1 tbsp. chopped cilantro leaves
1 tbsp. lime juice
1 small tomato, seeded
   and diced

SERVES 4

PREPARATION + COOKING
10 + 8 minutes + marinating

STORAGE
Leftovers will keep in the refrigerator up to 1 day.

SERVE THIS WITH...
mixed salad
Mango & Orange Fool
(see page 132)

HEALTH BENEFITS
Often shunned because of their high fat content, avocados are wonderful brain food, rich in essential B vitamins, folate, zinc, monounsaturated fats, and lecithin, a type of fat that plays a role in improving brain function.

1 Put the chicken between two sheets of plastic wrap and flatten with a rolling pin until very thin. Remove the plastic wrap and put the chicken in a dish. Mix together 2 tbsp. of the oil, the garlic, and jerk seasoning and pour it over the chicken. Cover and marinate in the refrigerator 30 minutes.
2 To make the guacamole, halve the avocado, remove the pit, and scoop the flesh into a bowl. Mash, using a fork, then mix in the remaining ingredients, cover, and chill.
3 Heat the remaining oil in a griddle pan. Sear the chicken 3 to 4 minutes on each side until charred and cooked through. Leave to cool 5 minutes, then slice thinly. Spread the guacamole on each roll bottom. Top with the chicken and sour cream. Replace the tops and serve.

chicken spring rolls

These delicious crispy rolls are baked, not fried, making them super healthy.

SERVES 4

PREPARATION + COOKING
10 + 25 minutes

STORAGE
Leftovers will keep in the refrigerator up to 1 day.

SERVE THIS WITH...
tomato salad
Almond Shortbread
  (see page 81)

HEALTH BENEFITS
Molasses is a great source of calcium, iron, B vitamins, magnesium, and manganese.

1 tbsp. olive oil, plus extra for
  brushing
4 scallions, finely sliced
1 garlic clove, crushed
2/3 cup tomato catsup
1 tbsp. honey
2 tsp. molasses

2 tsp. Worcestershire sauce
16 sheets of phyllo pastry
  dough, each 8 inches square
5 tbsp. olive oil
1½ cups shredded cooked
  chicken
2 tbsp. chopped cilantro leaves

1 Heat the oil in a pan. Add the scallions and garlic and cook 2 minutes, or until soft. Stir in the catsup, honey, molasses, and Worcestershire sauce. Simmer 2 minutes, or until thick, then remove from the heat.
2 Preheat the oven to 400°F. Lay a sheet of phyllo on a board with a corner facing you. Brush all over with oil, lay another sheet on top, and brush again with oil.
3 Lay a few strips of chicken toward the middle of the dough, top with a little sauce and cilantro, and fold the corner over the filling. Brush the sides with oil and fold them over the filling, then roll up. Repeat with the remaining phyllo and filling, then put on a baking sheet.
4 Brush with oil and bake 15 to 20 minutes until golden and crisp. Serve hot or cold.

Moroccan turkey wraps

Children will love the exotic flavors found in these fantastic wraps.

14 oz. skinless, boneless
   turkey breast, cut into strips
juice and zest of 1 lemon
¼ tsp. turmeric
½ tsp. each ground cumin,
   paprika, and ground
   coriander
3 tbsp. olive oil

4 oz. cherry tomatoes,
   quartered
1 roasted red bell pepper in oil,
   drained and sliced
4 large soft tortilla wraps
⅔ cup plain yogurt
2 tbsp. chopped cilantro leaves
½ romaine lettuce, shredded

1 Put the turkey in a shallow bowl. Mix together the lemon juice, zest, spices, and 2 tbsp. of the oil. Pour over the turkey, cover, and marinate at least 20 minutes.

2 Heat the remaining oil in a nonstick skillet and cook the turkey 6 to 8 minutes, stirring until golden brown and cooked through. Add the tomatoes and cook 1 to 2 minutes longer unil soft. Remove from the heat and stir in the bell pepper.

3 Heat the wraps according to the package directions. Mix the yogurt and cilantro in a small bowl. Divide the turkey and lettuce among the wraps and add a little of the cilantro yogurt. Fold over the bottoms of the wraps and roll up. Serve with the remaining cilantro yogurt.

SERVES 4

PREPARATION + COOKING
15 + 11 minutes + marinating

STORAGE
Leftovers will keep in the refrigerator up to 1 day.

SERVE THIS WITH...
carrot and celery sticks
fresh fruit
Lemon Oatmeal Cookies
  (see page 77)

HEALTH BENEFITS
Bright yellow turmeric contains an active constituent called curcumin, which is a powerful antioxidant that appears to protect brain cells from free-radical damage and inflammation, and in later life might help prevent mental decline.

028

⊙ ⊗ ⊛ ⊙ ⊛ ⊗

lamb & pea samosas

Samosas are a fun alternative to sandwiches and make a delicious portable snack.

MAKES 16

PREPARATION + COOKING
20 + 40 minutes

STORAGE
Leftovers will keep in the refrigerator up to 2 days.

SERVE THIS WITH...
vegetable sticks
Nut & Cherry Oat Bars
  (see page 86)

HEALTH BENEFITS
Peas are a fantastic superfood, containing vitamins B1, B2, B3, and B6, and folate, iron, and manganese. They also contain vitamin C, which is an important antioxidant.

1 tbsp.olive oil, plus extra
  for brushing
1 scallion, finely chopped
½ tsp. cinnamon
pinch of paprika
pinch of cayenne pepper
9 oz. ground lamb

1 tbsp. chopped mint
½ cup frozen peas
½ cup crumbled feta cheese
16 sheets of phyllo pastry
  dough, about 6¼ x 4½
  inches each

1 Heat the oil in a nonstick skillet. Add the scallion, cinnamon, paprika, and cayenne pepper, and cook, stirring, 1 minute. Add the lamb and cook 7 to 8 minutes until golden brown, stirring occasionally. Add the mint and peas and stir 1 minute to mix. Transfer to a bowl and add the feta.

2 Preheat the oven to 375°F. Brush a sheet of phyllo with oil and fold it in half lengthwise. Put a spoonful of meat at one end of the dough. Carefully fold the dough corner over the ground meat to form a triangle. Continue folding the triangle along the length of the strip to make a neat triangle shape. Repeat with the remaining phyllo sheets and filling.

3 Put the samosas on a baking sheet, brush the tops with olive oil, and bake 20 to 30 minutes until golden brown and crisp. Serve hot or cold.

steak ciabatta with avocado

Children will really perk up when they know this fantastic gourmet sandwich is for lunch.

4 sirloin steaks, 4 oz. each
1 red onion, sliced
1 garlic clove, crushed
2 thyme sprigs
4 tbsp. olive oil, plus extra
for drizzling

2 ciabatta loaves, halved
lengthwise
1 avocado
1 tomato, diced
1 tbsp. lemon juice
handful of baby spinach leaves

1 Put the steaks in a shallow dish. Add the onion, garlic, thyme, and oil to coat evenly. Cover and marinate 2 to 3 hours, or preferably overnight, in the refrigerator.
2 Preheat the oven to 350°F. Heat a skillet. Reserving the marinade, sear the steaks in the pan 3 minutes each side. Transfer to a plate and cover with foil.
3 Pour the marinade into the skillet and leave to cook 5 minutes, or until thick and the onion caramelizes.
4 Heat the ciabatta in the oven 5 minutes. Dice the avocado and mix it with the tomato and lemon juice.
5 Cut the steaks into thin strips. Drizzle each ciabatta with a little oil, then fill with the spinach, steak, caramelized onion, and avocado. Cut in half and serve.

SERVES 4

PREPARATION + COOKING
10 + 16 minutes + marinating

STORAGE
Leftovers will keep in the refrigerator up to 1 day.

SERVE THIS WITH...
coleslaw
Fruit Gels (see page 136)
Peanut Cookies (see page 80)

HEALTH BENEFITS
Red onions are a good source of chromium and also contain the antioxidants quercetin and vitamin C.

egg & tomato cups

Children love to help prepare this savory family favorite.

SERVES 4

PREPARATION + COOKING
15 + 25 minutes

STORAGE
Best eaten immediately.

SERVE THIS WITH...
green salad
Seeded Rye Bread
  (see page 74)
Pear, Blackberry & Walnut
  Crumble (see page 127)

HEALTH BENEFITS
Tomatoes are rich in lycopene, a powerful antioxidant that helps to maintain the health of the blood vessels that serve the brain. Lycopene is more readily available to our bodies, and more easily absorbed, from cooked and processed tomatoes than from raw ones.

olive oil, for greasing
4 large tomatoes
1 slice of lean cooked ham,
  about 1 oz., diced
4 tbsp. crème fraîche

1 tbsp. finely chopped parsley
  leaves
few drops of Tabasco sauce
4 eggs
freshly ground black pepper

1 Preheat the oven to 400°F and lightly grease a shallow baking dish with oil. Slice the top off each tomato and use a spoon to scoop out and discard the seeds and juice. Place, cut-sides down, on a piece of paper towel to drain.
2 In a bowl, mix together the ham, crème fraîche, and parsley and season with the Tabasco. Put the tomatoes in the dish, cut-sides up, and fill with the ham mixture.
3 Carefully crack 1 egg into each tomato and season with black pepper. Bake 20 to 25 minutes until the eggs are just set. Serve immediately.

Ⓥ ✗ ✗ Ⓞ ✗ ✗ ✗ ✗

baked stuffed peppers

This easy Mediterranean-style dish can be prepared in advance. The combination of dried fruit, lentils, and cheese makes a gorgeous filling that can also be used for stuffing large tomatoes or zucchini.

4 tbsp. raisins
1 tbsp. olive oil
1 red onion
1 garlic clove, crushed
3 sun-dried tomatoes in oil, drained and chopped
¾ cup cooked Puy lentils

4 tbsp. pine nuts
2 tbsp. chopped basil leaves
4 red bell peppers, halved and seeded
1¾ cup grated mozzarella cheese

SERVES 4

PREPARATION + COOKING
15 + 45 minutes

STORAGE
Leftovers will keep in the refrigerator up to 2 days.

SERVE THIS WITH...
mixed salad
Fruit Layer Crisp
(see page 134)

HEALTH BENEFITS
Puy lentils are a great source of folate and other B vitamins, zinc, and iron, and they are also rich in protein.

1 Preheat the oven to 350°F. Soak the raisins in just enough boiling water to cover 5 minutes; drain.
2 Heat the oil in a skillet and add the onion, garlic, and sun-dried tomatoes. Cook 2 to 3 minutes, stirring, until the onion is soft. Add the lentils, pine nuts, basil, and raisins and cook, stirring, 1 minute longer.
3 Put the peppers in a baking dish and spoon the lentil mixture into them. Top with the mozzarella cheese and bake 30 to 40 minutes until the peppers are soft and the cheese is bubbling and golden. Serve immediately.

032

Ⓥ Ⓧ Ⓧ Ⓧ Ⓧ Ⓧ Ⓧ Ⓧ Ⓧ

minted pea & cheese omelet

Omelets provide good-quality protein to fight off hunger pangs and guarantee plenty of brain energy for the afternoon. This recipe is perfect for a quick lunch or a brilliant weekend brunch.

SERVES 4

PREPARATION + COOKING
5 + 6 minutes

STORAGE
Best eaten immediately.

SERVE THIS WITH ...
Seeded Rye Bread
 (see page 74)
Mango & Orange Fool
 (see page 132)
cherry tomatoes
cucumber sticks

HEALTH BENEFITS
Mint is well known as a soothing herb for the gut. In particular, it helps to improve digestion so your child's body assimilates nutrients efficiently.

8 extra-large eggs
3 tbsp. chopped mint leaves
2 tbsp. olive oil
2 scallions, chopped
¾ cup frozen peas, defrosted

3 oz. goat cheese, chopped
2 tbsp. grated Parmesan
 cheese
freshly ground black pepper

1 Preheat the broiler to high. Beat the eggs with the mint and season with black pepper.

2 Heat the oil in a skillet with a flameproof handle. Add the scallions and cook 1 minute, then add the peas and stir 2 minutes. Pour in the eggs and cook 1 minute until they begin to set.

3 Scatter the goat cheese and Parmesan over the omelet and broil 2 minutes until light brown.

4 Slide the omelet onto a plate, cut it into wedges, and serve immediately.

cranberry & almond quinoa

Known as a "supergrain," quinoa is an excellent gluten-free alternative to pasta or couscous. Combined with fruit, nuts, and spices, it makes a great lunch-box meal.

1 cup quinoa
2 cups vegetable stock
pinch of saffron strands
1 tbsp. olive oil
1 red onion, chopped
1 garlic clove, crushed
½ cup dried cranberries
½ cup slivered almonds, toasted
½ cucumber, peeled, seeded, and diced
½ red bell pepper, seeded and diced
2 tbsp. lemon juice
2 tbsp. chopped cilantro leaves
2 tbsp. chopped mint leaves
1 preserved lemon, flesh and seeds removed, chopped
freshly ground black pepper

SERVES 4

PREPARATION + COOKING
15 + 25 minutes

STORAGE
Leftovers will keep in the refrigerator up to 2 days.

SERVE THIS WITH...
Apricot & Orange Soufflés (see page 125)
wholewheat pita bread

HEALTH BENEFITS
Quinoa is a complete protein and contains high levels of calcium, phosphorous, iron, B vitamins, and vitamin E, which protects the fatty membrane of brain cells.

1 Bring the quinoa, stock, and saffron to a boil. Reduce the heat, cover, and simmer 15 to 20 minutes until the water is absorbed. Transfer to a bowl to cool.
2 Heat the oil in a pan. Add the onion and garlic and fry 2 minutes, or until soft but not brown. Add to the quinoa with the remaining ingredients. Season with black pepper, mix well, and serve.

034

shrimp & mango tarts

These succulent tarts are bursting with flavor and healthy omega-3 essential fatty acids.

MAKES 8

PREPARATION + COOKING
15 + 14 minutes

STORAGE
Prepare the shrimp and mango mixture in advance and store it in the refrigerator to fill the tarts just before serving. Do not fill the tarts in advance.

SERVE THIS WITH...
green salad or coleslaw
Chocolate & Orange Mousse
(see page 131)

HEALTH BENEFITS
Mango is rich in the antioxidants vitamins C and E, betacarotene, and selenium, which all help to protect the body's cells.

4 tbsp. olive oil, plus extra for greasing
8 sheets of phyllo pastry dough, each 8 inches square
5 oz. shelled raw shrimp
2 tbsp. macadamia nuts, toasted and chopped
1 small mango, pitted and diced
2 roasted red bell peppers in oil, drained
1 tbsp. sweet chili sauce
2 tsp. tamari
1 tbsp. omega or flax-seed oil
1 tsp. lime juice

1 Preheat the oven to 400°F and grease eight cups in a muffin pan with oil. Reserve 1 tbsp. of the oil.
2 Brush 1 sheet of phyllo lightly with some of the remaining oil. Top with another sheet, brush again with oil, and cut into 2 double-thick squares to line the muffin-pan cups. Repeat with the remaining phyllo and oil.
3 Bake the tarts 8 to 10 minutes until crisp and golden. Turn out carefully onto a wire rack to cool.
4 Heat the reserved oil in a skillet and fry the shrimp 2 minutes on each side until pink. Put in a bowl with the nuts and mango.
5 Puree the remaining ingredients in a blender, then stir into the shrimp. Spoon the mixture into the tarts and serve.

Hong Kong shrimp

Better than a Chinese carry-out, this speedy shrimp dish is packed with energizing protein and protective antioxidants.

1 tbsp. olive oil
½-inch piece ginger root, peeled and grated
1 garlic clove, crushed
1 carrot, cut into matchstick strips
1 red bell pepper, seeded and cut into matchstick strips

20 jumbo shrimp, shelled and deveined
3 tbsp. tamari
2 tbsp. gluten-free oyster sauce
2 tbsp. Chinese rice wine
2 tbsp. chopped cilantro leaves

1 Heat a wok over medium heat. Add the oil and stir-fry the ginger, garlic, carrot, and pepper 1 minute. Add the shrimp and stir-fry 1 minute longer.

2 Stir in the tamari, oyster sauce, and rice wine and cook 3 to 4 minutes longer until the shrimp are cooked through and turn pink.

3 Sprinkle with the cilantro and serve.

SERVES 4

PREPARATION + COOKING
5 + 6 minutes

STORAGE
Leftovers will keep in the refrigerator up to 1 day.

SERVE THIS WITH
green beans
wilted spinach
Seeded Crackers (see page 72)
Tropical Crème Brûlée
  (see page 135)

HEALTH BENEFITS
Shrimp are an excellent source of selenium, which helps to keep the mind sharp and focused. They also provide brain-boosting omega-3 fats, energizing iron, and vitamin B12.

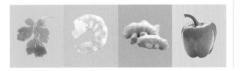

SERVES 4

PREPARATION + COOKING
15 + 25 minutes

STORAGE
Leftovers will keep in the
refrigerator up to 1 day.

SERVE THIS WITH ...
fresh fruit
Nut & Cherry Oat Bars
  (see page 86)

HEALTH BENEFITS
Anchovies might be small, but
they certainly pack a punch
in terms of brain-boosting
omega-3 fats.

salmon niçoise salad

Children love this colorful, nutrient-rich salad
for its lovely appearance and vibrant flavors.

6 new potatoes
3 oz.green beans
2 hearts of lettuces, leaves
    separated
6 oz. cherry tomatoes, halved
16 pitted black olives, halved
6 anchovy fillets, chopped
3 tsp. olive oil
4 salmon fillets, about
    3 oz. each
1 avocado

2 tsp. lime juice
4 hard-boiled eggs, quartered

Dressing:
1 tsp. Dijon mustard
2 tbsp. red-wine vinegar
pinch of sugar
6 tbsp. omega oil or
    flax-seed oil

1 Boil the potatoes 15 minutes, or until tender; drain and
halve. Meanwhile, cook the green beans 3 to 4 minutes until
they begin to soften, then drain. Put the potatoes, green
beans, lettuce leaves, tomatoes, olives, and anchovies in a
salad bowl and set aside.
2 Pour the oil over the salmon. Heat a griddle pan over
medium heat. Cook the salmon 4 to 5 minutes. Turn and
cook 1 minute, or until cooked through, then drain.
3 Slice the avocado and add it to the salad with the lime
juice and eggs. Whisk the dressing ingredients together,
pour it over the salad, and serve topped with the salmon.

sardine bruschetta with herb dressing

A popular Italian appetizer or snack, bruschetta topped with omega-boosting sardines and antioxidant-rich tomatoes makes a speedy and delicious lunch.

14 oz. canned sardines in
  olive oil
12 cherry tomatoes, halved
8 slices of ciabatta

Herb Dressing:
1 garlic clove, crushed
grated zest of 1 lemon
3 tbsp. lemon juice
4 tbsp. chopped parsley
5 tbsp. omega or flax-seed oil
freshly ground black pepper

1 Preheat the oven to 400°F. Drain the sardines, reserving 1 tbsp. of the oil, and put in a bowl. Put the tomatoes on a baking sheet, drizzle with the reserved oil, and bake 10 minutes, or until slightly soft.
2 Mix the dressing ingredients in a bowl and season with black pepper. Reserve 2 tbsp. of the dressing, then pour the rest over the sardines and break them up with a fork.
3 Add the tomatoes to the sardines and mix gently.
4 Lightly toast the bread. Drizzle with the reserved dressing, spoon on the sardine mixture. and serve immediately.

SERVES 4

PREPARATION + COOKING
15 + 12 minutes

STORAGE
Prepare the dressing in advance and keep it in an airtight container in the refrigerator up to 2 days. The bruschetta are best eaten immediately.

SERVE THIS WITH...
mixed salad
Fruity Phyllo Packages
  (see page 126)
Lemon Oatmeal Cookies
  (see page 77)

HEALTH BENEFITS
The omega or flax-seed oil in the dressing provides an easy boost to your child's daily intake of omega-3 fatty acids.

038

HEALTH BENEFITS
Fresh tuna is an excellent source of protein, selenium, and vitamin B12. It is also packed with EPA and DHA omega-3 essential fatty acids.

tuna kebabs with pineapple

This is a great dish for encouraging children to eat more oily fish. The refreshing pineapple relish provides a tangy accompaniment for the tuna. Try the kebabs on the barbecue, too.

10 oz. fresh tuna steak, cubed
1 red bell pepper, seeded and
   cut into chunks

Marinade:
juice of 2 oranges
2 tbsp. honey or agave nectar
2 tbsp. tamari

1 tbsp. olive oil

Pineapple Sambal:
2 oranges, peeled, segmented,
   and chopped
½ fresh pineapple, diced
1 scallion, finely chopped
3 tbsp. chopped cilantro leaves

SERVES 4

PREPARATION + COOKING
15 + 6 minutes + marinating

STORAGE
The sambal will keep in the
refrigerator up to 2 days. The
tuna kebabs are best cooked
and eaten on the day they are
prepared.

SERVE THIS WITH...
Summer Berry Pudding
  (see page 133)

1 Put the tuna in a shallow bowl. Stir the marinade
ingredients together in a small bowl and pour this over
the tuna. Cover with plastic wrap and chill 30 minutes.
Meanwhile, soak 8 wooden skewers in cold water.
2 To make the sambal, mix the oranges, pineapple,
scallion, and cilantro in a bowl, then cover with plastic
wrap and chill.
3 Thread the tuna and pepper chunks onto the skewers.
Pour the marinade from the tuna into a small pan and boil
1 to 2 minutes, then remove from the heat.
4 Preheat the broiler to high. Broil the kebabs
2 to 3 minutes on each side until brown and just cooked.
Put 2 kebabs on each plate and drizzle some of the
marinade. Serve with a portion of sambal on the side.

**Pineapple aids
digestion, provides
energy, balances
blood-sugar levels,
and protects brain
cells from damage.**

Thai chicken salad

This fresh and crunchy salad is rather like an oriental version of coleslaw, with vibrant-colored vegetables for antioxidant protection and chicken for low-fat protein.

SERVES 4

PREPARATION
15 minutes

STORAGE
Leftovers will keep in the refrigerator up to 1 day.

SERVE THIS WITH...
Mango & Orange Fool
  (see page 132)
Almond Shortbread
  (see page 81)
couscous

HEALTH BENEFITS
Bright-colored salads are full of antioxidants, including betacarotene and vitamins C and E.

2 cooked skinless, boneless
  chicken breast halves,
  shredded
1 carrot, cut into fine strips
1 red bell pepper, seeded and
  cut into fine strips
¼ small white cabbage,
  shredded
3 scallions, finely chopped
4 shiitake mushrooms, sliced

1¾ oz. bean sprouts
2 tbsp. chopped mint
2 tbsp. chopped cilantro leaves

Dressing:
2 tsp. fish sauce
2 tbsp. lime juice
2 tbsp. honey or agave nectar
2 tsp. tamari
1 tbsp. omega or flax-seed oil

1 Layer the chicken, carrot, pepper, cabbage, scallions, mushrooms, and bean sprouts in a large bowl. Sprinkle with the mint and cilantro.
2 Whisk the dressing ingredients in a small bowl, then pour over the salad. Toss lightly and serve.

pork & egg-fried rice

This dish has it all: protein-rich eggs and pork, brown basmati rice for stable blood-sugar levels, and loads of nutritious veggies.

1 cup brown basmati rice
3 tbsp. olive oil
9 oz. lean ground pork
2 eggs, beaten
2 tsp. sesame oil
2 scallions, finely chopped
2 tomatoes, chopped
½ cup frozen peas
½ red bell pepper, seeded and diced
2 tbsp. tamari
handful of cilantro leaves, chopped
freshly ground black pepper

1 Cook the rice according to the package directions until tender; drain and cool.

2 Heat a wok or large skillet and add 1 tbsp. of the olive oil. Add the pork and stir-fry 5 to 6 minutes until brown and cooked. Transfer to a bowl and set aside.

3 Heat half the remaining olive oil in the wok. Beat the eggs with half the sesame oil, then pour them into the wok and cook 1 to 2 minutes, stirring, until scrambled and lightly set. Transfer to a warm plate.

4 Heat the remaining oil in the wok. Stir-fry the rice, scallions, tomatoes, peas, and pepper 1 to 2 minutes. Add the pork, egg, and tamari and stir 2 to 3 minutes longer until hot. Season with black pepper, sprinkle with the cilantro and serve.

SERVES 4

PREPARATION + COOKING
15 + 40 minutes

STORAGE
Leftovers will keep in the refrigerator up to 1 day.
If reheating, make sure the rice is piping hot before serving.

SERVE THIS WITH …
mixed salad
Tropical Crème Brûlée
(see page 135)

HEALTH BENEFITS
Brown basmati rice has a low GI score and, unlike more-refined white rice, is rich in minerals and vitamins, including manganese, selenium, magnesium, and B vitamins.

041

SERVES 4

PREPARATION + COOKING
15 + 18 minutes

STORAGE
Best eaten immediately.

SERVE THIS WITH...
green salad
Pineapple & Mint Frozen Yogurt
(see page 138)

HEALTH BENEFITS
Beans are a good source
of fiber. Kidney beans, in
particular, are rich in iron,
folate, and magnesium, and
they also supply thiamine
(vitamin B1), needed for the
synthesis of acetylcholine,
the neurotransmitter that is
essential for memory.

avocado with savory crumbs

This simple, energizing dish is bursting with
flavor and healthy fats to support brain health
and keep kids focused.

1 tbsp. olive oil, plus extra for
   greasing
2 bacon slices
1 slice of wholewheat bread
½ cup grated cheddar cheese

2 avocados, halved lengthwise
   and pitted, shells reserved
1 cup canned refried beans
4 cherry tomatoes, quartered

1 Preheat the broiler to high and the oven to 400°F. Lightly
grease a baking dish with oil.
2 Broil the bacon 2 to 3 minutes until crisp. Crumble the
bacon into a bowl when cool.
3 Process the bread to fine crumbs in a food processor.
Put in a bowl and mix in the olive oil and half the cheese.
4 Dice the avocado flesh or mash it with a fork and mix
with the beans, tomatoes, remaining cheese, and bacon.
5 Spoon the bean mixture into the avocado shells and
place them in the prepared dish. Sprinkle with the
crumbs, press down lightly, and bake 10 to 15 minutes
until golden. Serve immediately.

quick & easy bean & ham salad

This light, summery salad uses pantry ingredients and can be assembled in minutes.

3 tbsp. olive oil
2 scallions, chopped
2 garlic cloves, crushed
½ red chili, seeded
   and chopped
2 tomatoes, seeded
   and chopped
1 can (15-oz.) cannellini beans,
   drained and rinsed

1 can (15-oz.) lima beans,
   drained and rinsed
2 tbsp. flax-seed oil
2 tbsp. lemon juice
3 tbsp. chopped parsley leaves
3 oz. lean cooked ham, cut
   into slivers

1 Heat 1 tbsp.of the olive oil in a skillet and sauté the scallins, garlic, and chili 1 minute, or until soft. Toss in the tomatoes and beans and warm through 2 minutes, then transfer to a bowl.

2 Whisk together the remaining olive oil, flax-seed oil, lemon juice, and parsley. Toss through the salad, scatter the ham on top, and serve.

SERVES 4

PREPARATION + COOKING
10 + 3 minutes

STORAGE
Leftovers will keep in the refrigerator up to 4 days.

SERVE THIS WITH ...
Seeded Rye Bread
   (see page 74)
Tomato & Chickpea Soup
   (see page 44)

HEALTH BENEFITS
Canned beans are an excellent source of protein and fiber.

SNACKS

A midmorning or midafternoon snack helps balance blood-sugar levels, providing ample energy to stay alert and attentive. There is no reason to ban crackers, brownies, cookies, and cakes because it is easy to make terrific treats for children using whole grains, nuts, seeds, and fresh and dried fruit. The recipes in this chapter are low in refined sugar, but are full of brain-boosting nutrients and slow-release carbohydrates, along with protein to avoid the highs and lows that often result from eating sugary cookies or candy. Many, such as Chocolate & Cranberry Brownies, Almond Shortbread, and Banana & Mango Cake, are perfect for packed lunches or are sufficiently special for parties. For savory snacks, why not bake a batch of Pumpkin Biscuits or some Seeded Rye Bread?

Ⓥ ⓘ ⓧ ⓨ ⓧ

hummus & seeded crackers

This is a delicious alternative to store-bought dips, and the crackers are rich in calcium and slow-release carbohydrates.

SERVES 6

PREPARATION + COOKING
10 + 10 minutes

STORAGE
The hummus will keep in the refrigerator up to 4 days or in the freezer up to 1 month. Store the crackers in an airtight container up to 2 days.

SERVE THIS WITH ...
vegetable sticks, including bell peppers, cucumber, carrot, snow peas, and baby corn cobs

HEALTH BENEFITS
Chickpeas are an excellent source of protein and soluble fiber. They also contain the minerals iron, magnesium, zinc, and manganese.

1 can (15-oz.) chickpeas,
    drained and rinsed
2 sun-dried tomatoes in oil,
    drained
1 tbsp. lemon juice
2 garlic cloves, crushed
1 tbsp. tahini
3 tbsp. flax-seed or hemp-
    seed oil

pinch of paprika

Seeded Crackers:
3 wholewheat pita breads,
    halved lengthwise
2 tbsp. olive oil
3 tbsp. sesame seeds
pinch of paprika
2 tbsp. Parmesan cheese

1 Preheat the oven to 400°F. Bake the crackers first. Brush the pitas with the oil and cut them into small triangles. Put on a baking sheet, sprinkle with the seeds, paprika, and Parmesan. Bake 5 to 10 minutes until golden brown and crisp. Cool on a rack 2 to 3 minutes.

2 Process the chickpeas, tomatoes, lemon juice, garlic, and tahini in a food processor or blender to form a thick paste. Add the oil and process until smooth and creamy.

3 Spoon the hummus into a bowl and sprinkle with the paprika. Serve with the seeded crackers.

(V) (X) (X) (X)

pumpkin biscuits

These golden biscuits are fabulous straight from the oven and are a perfect snack or accompaniment for soups and stews.

2 tbsp. olive oil, plus extra for
    greasing
1 cup wholewheat flour
1 cup self-rising flour, plus
    extra for rolling the dough
½ tsp. baking powder
pinch of cayenne pepper
¼ tsp. mustard powder

3 tbsp. sesame seeds
¾ cup canned unsweetened
    pumpkin puree
½ cup crumbled feta cheese
1 egg, beaten
milk, for brushing

1 Preheat the oven to 400°F and lightly grease a baking sheet with oil. Sift the flours into a large bowl. Stir in the baking powder, cayenne pepper, mustard powder, and 2 tbsp. of the sesame seeds.

2 Make a well in the dry ingredients. Add the oil, pumpkin puree, and feta, then stir in the egg. Gradually mix to form a soft dough. Lightly knead the dough into a smooth ball and roll out on a floured surface to 1 inch thick.

3 Use a 2-inch cutter to stamp out 10 to 12 biscuits, rerolling as necessary. Put them on the baking sheet, brush with milk, and sprinkle with the remaining sesame seeds. Bake 12 to 15 minutes until risen and golden. Cool on a wire rack, then serve.

MAKES 10 TO 12

PREPARATION AND COOKING
10 + 15 minutes

STORAGE
Store in an airtight container in the refrigerator up to 3 days or in the freezer up to 1 month.

SERVE THIS WITH...
Tomato & Chickpea Soup
  (see page 44)

HEALTH BENEFITS
Pumpkin is bursting with antioxidants, including betacarotene, vitamins E and C, and vital B vitamins.

045

Ⓥ ⓐ Ⓠ Ⓧ Ⓒ Ⓧ

seeded rye bread

This nutty bread is a great afternoon pick-me-up.

MAKES 1 LOAF

PREPARATION AND COOKING
15 + 35 minutes + proving

STORAGE
Wrap and store in an airtight
container up to 2 days or in the
freezer up to 1 month.

SERVE THIS WITH...
Hummus (see page 72)
a poached egg

HEALTH BENEFITS
Rye is a rich source of
magnesium and fiber and also
contains B vitamins.

2¾ cups wholewheat bread
    flour, plus extra for kneading
    the dough
1¼ cups light rye flour
1 tsp. salt
2 envelopes fast-acting
    dry yeast

½ cup sunflower seeds
½ cup pumpkin seeds
3 tbsp. flax seeds
5 tbsp. sesame seeds
3 tbsp. molasses
1 tbsp. honey or agave nectar
olive oil, for greasing

1 Put the flours, salt, yeast, and sunflower, pumpkin, and
flax seeds in a large bowl. Mix in 2 tbsp. of the sesame
seeds and make a well in the middle.

2 Mix the molasses and honey with 1¼ cups warm
water and add to the flour. Stir to form a stiff dough, then
knead 10 minutes on a floured surface. Put in a bowl,
cover with plastic wrap, and leave to rise 1 hour, or until
doubled in size.

3 Grease a baking sheet with oil. Knead the dough briefly,
shape into a round, and put on the sheet. Score the top
with a knife, brush with water, and sprinkle with the
remaining sesame seeds. Cover with plastic wrap and leave
to rise 30 minutes. Preheat the oven to 400°F.

4 Bake 30 to 35 minutes until golden and hollow-
sounding when tapped underneath. Cool on a wire rack
before serving.

Ⓥ Ⓧ Ⓧ Ⓧ Ⓧ

raisin French toast

This is an irresistible, sweet sandwich dipped in egg and fried. Adding a few raisins to the filling is a great way to restore your child's flagging energy levels.

3 eggs, beaten
4 tbsp. crème fraîche
1 tsp. cinnamon
2 ripe peaches, pitted
¼ cup raisins
8 slices of wholewheat bread
1 tbsp. butter
1 tbsp. olive oil

1 In a large bowl, whisk the eggs with the crème fraîche and cinnamon until frothy.
2 Puree the peaches in a blender, then mix in the raisins. Spread the puree on half the bread slices and top with the remaining slices to make sandwiches.
3 Melt the butter with the olive oil in a large skillet. Dip a sandwich into the egg mixture and turn it a couple of times to make sure it is well soaked. Fry 1 to 2 minutes on each side until golden and crisp; repeat with remaining sandwiches. Cut into triangles and serve immediately.

SERVES 4

PREPARATION AND COOKING
10 + 16 minutes

STORAGE
Best eaten immediately.

SERVE THIS WITH...
a glass of freshly squeezed orange juice

HEALTH BENEFITS
Cinnamon is useful for regulating blood-sugar levels.

MAKES 1 LOAF

PREPARATION AND COOKING
20 + 35 minutes + proving

STORAGE
Wrap and store in the
refrigerator up to 3 days or in the
freezer up to 1 month.

SERVE THIS WITH …
Tomato & Chickpea Soup
(see page 44)
a boiled egg

HEALTH BENEFITS
Nut and seed breads are a great
source of protein, essential fats,
vitamins (including vitamin E),
and minerals, such as calcium,
magnesium, and zinc—a great
combination for brain health.
Wholewheat flour provides a
steady supply of glucose to
the brain to avoid dips in
concentration.

Ⓥ Ⓒ ⊘ ✪

cheese & walnut bread

Toasted and served with soup, this bread
makes a satisfying light meal.

scant 2½ cups wholewheat
    bread flour
1⅔ cups white bread flour, plus
    extra for kneading the dough
2 envelopes fast-acting dry
    yeast

1 tsp. salt
½ cup walnuts, chopped
⅔ cup grated cheddar cheese
1 tbsp. olive oil, plus extra for
    greasing
milk, for brushing

1 Mix the flours, yeast, and salt in a large bowl. Stir in the
walnuts and cheese. Make a well in the middle and add
the oil and 1¼ cups warm water, then mix to form
a soft dough.

2 Turn the dough out onto a lightly floured surface and
knead 10 minutes. Put in a bowl, cover with plastic wrap,
and leave to rise 1 hour, or until double in size.

3 Grease a baking sheet. Knead the dough briefly, shape
it into a round loaf and put it on the baking sheet. Cover
and leave to rise 20 minutes, or until double in size.

4 Preheat the oven to 400°F. Brush the loaf with milk and
bake 30 to 35 minutes until golden brown. When baked,
the loaf will sound hollow when tapped underneath. Cool
on a wire rack, then serve.

(V) (×) (○) (×) (○)

lemon oatmeal cookies

These delightful cookies are easy to make and shape—so ask for some help from tiny hands!

1 lemon
grated zest of 2 lemons
¾ cup chopped dates
2 tbsp. butter
¼ cup rolled oats

1 cup steel-cut oats
1 tbsp. ground flax seeds
rice flour, for shaping the
    cookies

MAKES 8

PREPARATION AND COOKING
10 + 20 minutes

STORAGE
Store in an airtight container
up to 3 days.

SERVE THIS WITH ...
fresh fruit
Peach & Almond Rice Pudding
(see page 124)

HEALTH BENEFITS
Dates provide sweetness but
also plenty of fiber, B vitamins,
and minerals, including iron,
manganese, and magnesium.

1 Preheat the oven to 350°F and line a baking sheet with baking parchment.
2 Peel the lemon and cut the flesh into bite-size pieces, discarding the seeds. Place in a saucepan with the grated zest, dates, and butter. Heat slowly 1 minute, or until the butter melts, then puree in a food processor.
3 Put the rolled oats, steel-cut oats, and flax seeds in a bowl. Stir in the puree to form a soft dough. With floured hands, divide the dough into 8 equal pieces and flatten them into cookie shapes.
4 Place on the baking sheet and bake 15 to 20 minutes until golden. Cool on a wire rack, then serve.

Ⓥ 🐾 ✂ ❄ 🥜

flax-seed gingerbread men

HEALTH BENEFITS
Flax seeds are full of omega-3 fatty acids: important for brain development and function. They are also high in fiber to aid digestion and help to stabilize blood-sugar levels.

This wonderfully healthy gingerbread recipe is simple enough to get children involved with the baking. Cut out gingerbread men or use any cutters you have. The result is a spicy treat for packed lunches or snack time.

½ cup tahini
½ cup ground flax seeds
4 tbsp. honey or agave nectar
1 egg, beaten, plus extra for
    glazing
1 cup all-purpose or
    wholewheat flour, plus extra
    for rolling the dough

1 tsp. cinnamon
1½ tsp. ground ginger
¼ tsp. baking soda
olive oil, for greasing

1 In a bowl, mix the tahini, flax seeds, honey, and egg
and beat until creamy and smooth.
2 In another bowl, sift together the flour, cinnamon,
ginger, and baking soda. Add the tahini mixture and mix
well to form a stiff dough. Knead lightly, wrap in plastic
wrap, and chill 15 minutes.
3 Preheat the oven to 350°F and lightly grease a baking
sheet with oil. Lightly flour a work surface and roll out
the dough to about ½ inch thick. Using a cookies cutter,
stamp out 12 to 14 shapes. Place them on the baking
sheet and brush with a little beaten egg.
4 Bake 10 to 12 minutes until a pale golden brown.
Leave to cool on the baking sheet 5 minutes, then
transfer to a wire rack to cool completely before serving.

MAKES 12 TO 14

PREPARATION + COOKING
15 + 12 minutes + chilling

STORAGE
Store in an airtight container
up to 4 days. Freeze the dough
up to 3 months.

SERVE THIS WITH ...
vegetable sticks
fresh fruit
Griddled Chicken & Guacamole
  Rolls (see page 51)

Tahini provides
essential omega-6
fatty acids plus
brain-boosting
zinc, calcium, and
magnesium.

050

MAKES 10 TO 12

PREPARATION AND COOKING
10 + 15 minutes

STORAGE
Store in an airtight container
up to 4 days.

SERVE THIS WITH ...
handful of dried fruit
apple slices

HEALTH BENEFITS
Sesame seeds are a rich source
of omega-6 essential fatty acids
and also contain protein, zinc,
calcium, and magnesium.

peanut cookies

These cookies will disappear before your eyes.

3 tbsp. + 1 tsp. unsalted butter,
    plus extra for greasing
½ cup crunchy peanut butter
1 tsp. cinnamon
3 tbsp. honey or agave nectar
heaped ½ cup rolled oats

1 tbsp. ground flax seeds
¾ cup shredded coconut
1 tsp. vanilla extract
1 cup wholewheat flour
2 tbsp. sesame seeds
2 eggs, beaten

1 Preheat the oven to 350°F and grease and line a baking
sheet. Gently heat the peanut butter, butter, cinnamon,
and honey in a pan until the butter melts. Stir in the oats,
flax seeds, coconut, vanilla extract, flour, and sesame
seeds. Add the eggs and mix well.
2 Drop 10 to 12 spoonfuls of the dough well apart
on the baking sheet and press down into circles. Bake
10 to 12 minutes until light brown. Leave on the sheet
5 minutes. Place on a wire rack to cool, then serve.

(V) (X) (X) (X) (X) (X)

almond shortbread

This buttery shortbread is a great addition
to packed lunches or as an after-school treat.

4 tbsp. unsalted butter, plus
extra for greasing
scant 1 cup rice flour, plus
extra (optional) for rolling
the dough

1½ cups finely ground almonds
¼ cup superfine sugar
4 tbsp. almond butter
1 egg plus 1 egg yolk, beaten

1 Preheat the oven to 350ºF and grease a round 8-inch
loose-bottomed, shallow pan with butter.
2 Put the rice flour and almonds in a large bowl. Melt the
sugar, butter, and almond butter in a small pan and pour
it into the almond mixture. Add the egg and yolk and mix
to form a soft dough. Press the dough into the pan.
3 Alternatively, to make small shortbreads, wrap the
dough in plastic wrap and chill 20 minutes. Roll out
on a floured surface and cut into 8 circles, using a 2½-
to 3¼-inch cutter. Put on a greased baking sheet.
4 Bake the shortbreads 20 minutes, or until golden
brown. Cool the large ones completely in the pan, cutting
into wedges after about 10 minutes. Transfer the small
ones to a wire rack to cool completely, then serve.

MAKES 8

PREPARATION AND COOKING
10 + 20 minutes + chilling
(optional)

STORAGE
Store in an airtight container
up to 3 days. Freeze the dough
up to 1 month.

SERVE THIS WITH ...
Fruit Gels (see pages 136)
fresh strawberries and
raspberries
plain yogurt

HEALTH BENEFITS
Almonds are an excellent
source of monounsaturated
fats and protein, which helps
to keep energy levels stable.
This recipe also contains calming
magnesium and calcium, as well
as iron, zinc, and vitamin E.

Ⓥ Ⓧ Ⓧ Ⓞ Ⓞ Ⓞ

tahini chocolate fudge

Cut into small pieces, these melt-in-the-mouth morsels are perfect for parties or as a healthy treat when your child's focus is wavering.

MAKES 30 TO 36 PIECES

PREPARATION + CHILLING
15 minutes + 3 hours

STORAGE
Store in the refrigerator
up to 1 week or in the freezer
up to 1 month.

SERVE THIS WITH...
Apricot & Tofu Boost
(see page 22)

HEALTH BENEFITS
Almonds and sesame seeds are
rich in calcium and magnesium:
two wonderfully calming
minerals that help to balance
mood and create a restful sleep.

¼ cup sesame seeds
1⅓ cups almonds
6 dates, chopped
½ tsp. cinnamon
2 tbsp. shredded coconut
1 tbsp. ground flax seeds

6 tbsp. tahini
6 tbsp. honey or agave nectar
5 oz. semisweet chocolate,
    melted
olive oil, for greasing

1 Put the sesame seeds and almonds in a food processor and process until finely ground. Add the dates, cinnamon, coconut, and flax seeds and process to form a coarse paste. Transfer the mixture to a bowl.
2 Mix the tahini, honey, and chocolate until blended. Add to the almonds and stir well to form a sticky dough.
3 Lightly grease and line a 13- x 8-inch pan with oil and press the mixture into the pan. Chill in the refrigerator 2 to 3 hours until firm, then cut into 30 to 36 small pieces and serve.

(V) 🐟 🥜 🌿 🥚

chocolate fruit truffles

Treat your children to these amazing morsels that combine irresistible dark chocolate with nutrient-packed nuts and dried fruit.

¾ cup chopped dried apricots
½ cup chopped dates
3½ oz. dark chocolate, melted (75% cocoa solids)
2 tbsp. ground flax seeds

2 tbsp. sesame seeds
4 tbsp. ground almonds
2 tbsp. chopped mixed nuts or shredded coconut, for coating

1 Process the apricots, dates, and chocolate in a food processor to form a thick paste. Add the flax seeds, sesame seeds, and almonds and stir until a stiff, sticky dough forms.
2 Roll the mixture into 10 to 12 small balls and roll them in the chopped nuts or coconut to coat. Chill 30 minutes, or until firm, then serve.

MAKES 10 TO 12

PREPARATION + CHILLING
15 + 30 minutes

STORAGE
Keep in the refrigerator up to 4 days.

SERVE THIS WITH ...
slices of fresh fruit

HEALTH BENEFITS
Chocolate is a brain food but not in its sweet, processed form. Instead, look for bars containing at least 75% cocoa solids. Rich in brain-stimulating chemicals such as theobromine, tyramine, and phenylethylamine, chocolate can improve alertness, reduce depression, and boost cognitive performance.

Ⓥ ⊘ ⊘ ⊘ ⊘

chocolate & cranberry brownies

Healthy brownies? Yes! Prunes replace the fat and most of the sugar used in other recipes.

MAKES 10 TO 12

PREPARATION + COOKING
15 + 30 minutes

STORAGE
Store in the refrigerator up to 4 days or in the freezer up to 3 months, then defrost in the refrigerator overnight.

SERVE THIS WITH...
Fruit Gels (see page 136)
fresh raspberries

HEALTH BENEFITS
Not only a great source of fiber, prunes are also a concentrated source of the antioxidant vitamins A and C, B vitamins, iron, and potassium.

olive oil, for greasing
heaped ½ cup pitted prunes
¼ cup sugar
4 oz. dark chocolate, chopped (75% cocoa solids)
¾ cup dried cranberries
¼ cup chopped pecans
1 tsp. vanilla extract
½ cup wholewheat flour
1 tsp. baking powder
scant ¼ cup wheat germ
3 eggs, separated

1 Preheat the oven to 350ºF and grease and line the bottom of a square 6-inch cake pan. Blend the prunes, sugar, and 3 tbsp. water in a blender.

2 Melt the chocolate in a bowl over a pan of simmering water. Remove from the heat and stir in the prunes, cranberries, pecans, vanilla extract, flour, baking powder, wheat germ, and egg yolks.

3 Whisk the egg whites until they form soft peaks and, with a metal spoon, fold them into the chocolate mixture.

4 Spoon the batter into the pan. Bake 20 to 25 minutes until risen and firm to touch. Leave in the pan to cool. Cut into 10 to 12 squares and serve.

(V) (icons)

apricot muesli bars

Fruity and moist, these super-healthy bars will give your child's depleted blood-sugar levels a gentle, steady boost.

²/₃ cup light olive oil or canola oil, plus extra for greasing
2¾ cups dried apricots
1¼ cups unsweetened muesli or rolled oats
1 cup wholewheat flour
½ cup mixed seeds

1 tsp. cinnamon
1 cup finely ground almonds
¾ cup shredded coconut
2 oranges, peeled, seeds removed
5 tbsp. honey or agave nectar

MAKES 14 TO 16

PREPARATION AND COOKING
15 + 30 minutes

STORAGE
Store in an airtight container in the refrigerator up to 4 days.

SERVE THIS WITH ...
vegetable sticks
fresh orange segments
fresh mixed berries
Hummus & Seeded Crackers
  (see page 72)
Pineapple & Mint Frozen Yogurt
  (see page 138)

HEALTH BENEFITS
Dried apricots contain good amounts of iron, which aids learning and memory. The vitamin C in the apricots—and the oranges—helps the body to absorb iron from food.

1 Preheat the oven to 350°F and lightly grease a shallow 12- x 8-inch pan with oil. Chop 1 cup of the apricots and mix them with the muesli, flour, seeds, cinnamon, almonds, and coconut in a large bowl.

2 Puree the remaining apricots with the oranges, honey, and oil in a food processor or blender. Add the puree to the oat mixture and stir until thoroughly combined.

3 Spread the mixture evenly in the prepared pan and bake 25 to 30 minutes until golden. Leave to cool in the pan, cutting it into 14 to 16 bars while still warm, then serve.

nut & cherry oat bars

These moist, gooey bars will prove irresistibly good to the whole family.

MAKES 12–14

PREPARATION AND COOKING
15 + 30 minutes

STORAGE
Store in an airtight container up to 3 days.

SERVE THIS WITH ...
fresh vanilla custard sauce
Creamy Salmon & Alfalfa Pitas
(see page 49)

HEALTH BENEFITS
Cherries are exceptionally rich in antioxidants, including betacarotene and vitamins C and E. They also contain magnesium, folate, and iron, which promote brain health, and are one of the few food sources of melatonin—useful for maintaining children's natural sleep patterns.

olive oil, for greasing
1 cup dates
1 cup cashew nuts, soaked
  in water overnight and
  drained
¾ cup apple juice

3 tbsp. honey or agave nectar
scant 2 cups rolled oats
3 tbsp. sesame seeds
3 tbsp. sunflower seeds
3 tbsp. ground flax seeds
²⁄₃ cup dried cherries

1 Preheat the oven to 350°F and grease and line a shallow 13- x 8-inch baking pan with oil.
2 Process the dates, cashews, apple juice, and honey in a food processor or blender to form a smooth puree.
3 Put the oats, seeds, and dried cherries in a large bowl. Add the puree and stir to combine thoroughly. Spread the mixture in the prepared pan.
4 Bake 25 to 30 minutes until golden brown. Leave to cool 10 minutes, then cut into 12 to 14 bars while still warm. Leave in the pan until completely cool, then serve.

Ⓥ ⓧ ⓧ ⓧ ⓧ ⓧ

blueberry muffins

Fun to make with your children, these little muffins are packed with natural sweetness. The wholewheat flour is a great source of complex carbohydrates to help steady blood-sugar levels and maintain focus all day.

5 tbsp. olive oil, plus extra for
   greasing
2 cups wholewheat flour
2 tsp. baking powder
2 eggs, beaten

5 tbsp. milk
2 bananas, mashed
heaped 1 cup blueberries

1 Preheat the oven to 400°F and grease 8 to 10 cups of a muffin pan with oil. Sift the flour and baking powder into a bowl. In another bowl, beat the eggs, oil, and milk and stir in the bananas. Pour the wet mixture into the flour and mix well. Fold in the blueberries.
2 Spoon the batter into the muffin cups and bake 15 to 20 minutes until risen, firm to the touch, and golden.
3 Turn out onto a wire rack to cool, then serve.

MAKES 8 TO 10

PREPARATION AND COOKING
10 + 20 minutes

STORAGE
Store in an airtight container in the refrigerator up to 3 days or in the freezer up to 1 month.

SERVE THIS WITH ...
plain yogurt
Mango & Orange Fool
  (see page 132)

HEALTH BENEFITS
Blueberries are rich in anthocyanins and have been shown to improve brain function.

HEALTH BENEFITS
Bananas are rich in B vitamins, especially B6. Together with the amino acid tryptophan, B6 can be converted by the body into the calming hormone serotonin, which can help to relieve stress and anxiety. Bananas are also excellent energizers. When combined with slow-release carbohydrates, such as wholewheat flour, they provide plenty of brain fuel.

banana & mango cake

A tropical twist on an all-time favorite, this recipe is far lower in sugar than traditional banana cakes. It uses plenty of fresh and dried fruit, with wholewheat flour rich in B vitamins, fiber, magnesium, and selenium to boost energy levels and keep the mind sharp.

1 stick butter, melted,
   plus extra for greasing
1 cup chopped dried mango
1½ cups wholewheat self-rising
   flour
½ cup shredded coconut
2 tsp. baking powder
1 tsp. ground cinnamon
3 bananas, mashed

2 eggs
¼ cup sugar
handful of dried banana chips

Filling:
9 oz. cream cheese
1½ tbsp. honey or agave nectar
½ mango, peeled, pitted, and
   finely chopped

MAKES AB 8-INCH CAKE

PREPARATION + COOKING
15 + 40 minutes

STORAGE
Store in the refrigerator up
to 3 days.

SERVE THIS WITH ...
slices of fresh mango
plain yogurt
Turkey Noodle Soup
   (see page 43)

1 Preheat the oven to 350°F and grease a 8-inch deep cake pan with butter. Cover the dried mango with boiling water and soak 10 minutes, then drain.

2 Mix the flour, coconut, baking powder, and cinnamon in a bowl. Stir in the dried mango. Blend the melted butter, bananas, eggs, and sugar in a blender until smooth. Add to the flour and mix well. Spoon the batter into the pan and top with the bananas chips. Bake 30 to 40 minutes until firm and golden. Cool completely on a wire rack.

3 Beat the cream cheese and honey. Stir in the mango. Slice the cake in half horizontally, spread the filling in the middle, and sandwich it back together, then serve.

Dried fruit is
a good source of
vitamins and
minerals. Look for
dried fruit without
added sugar.

DINNERS

Family meals are a great time to unwind together after a busy day, and this chapter includes a variety of dishes to appeal to the whole family. There are healthier versions of "junk foods" for fussy eaters. Try, for example, Sesame-Polenta Chicken Strips, Tex-Mex Burgers, Turkey Meatballs in Five-Veg Sauce, or Salmon Fishcakes. Family-style comfort food includes Creamy Fish Pie, Sweet & Sour Chicken, and Bean & Sausage Hotpot. Vegetarians will absolutely love Barley Risotto. All the recipes have been developed to maximize their nutrient content, with brain-boosting fats, vitamins, minerals, and protein partnered by slow-release carbohydrates to balance energy with relaxation and encourage better sleep.

spicy fish tacos

SERVES 4

PREPARATION + COOKING
10 + 7 minutes

STORAGE
Leftovers will keep in the
refrigerator up to 1 day.

SERVE THIS WITH ...
green beans
Pineapple & Mint Frozen Yogurt
(see page 138)

HEALTH BENEFITS
White fish is a good source of
low-fat protein needed for the
production of neurotransmitters
in the brain. It also has plenty
of B vitamins to help the body
release energy from foods.

Children love finger food, and these lightly
spiced fish tacos will be a big hit. Use firm
white fish from sustainable sources.

1 avocado, diced
2 tsp. lemon juice
14 oz. skinless, boneless firm
white fish fillets, such as
halibut
¼ cup all-purpose flour
1 tbsp. olive oil
3 tomatoes, seeded and diced
1 cup canned kidney beans,
drained and rinsed
1 tbsp. sweet chili sauce
1 tbsp. tamari
1 tbsp. rice wine
1 tsp. sugar
8 taco shells
freshly ground black pepper

1 Mix the avocado and lemon juice in a bowl; cover and chill.
2 Cut the fish fillets into thick strips and dry on paper
towels. Put the flour in a bowl, season with black pepper,
and toss the fish strips in it.
3 Heat a large skillet and add the oil. Stir-fry the fish
3 to 4 minutes until crisp and golden. Stir in the tomatoes,
kidney beans, chili sauce, tamari, rice wine, and sugar and
simmer 1 to 2 minutes until the tomatoes are soft.
4 Heat the taco shells according to the package directions.
Fill with the fish and beans and top with a spoonful
of avocado, then serve.

seafood kebabs

This is the perfect way to get your children to eat more seafood—and boost their intake of omega-3 fatty acids.

2 tbsp. olive oil
2 tsp. paprika
4 tbsp. sun-dried tomato paste
4 tbsp. lime juice
2 tbsp. honey or agave nectar
12 raw jumbo shrimp, shelled
   and deveined

8 oz. monkfish fillet, gray
   membrane removed and cut
   into chunks
8 oz. skinless, boneless trout
   fillets, cut into chunks
1 red and 1 yellow bell pepper,
   seeded and cut into chunks

SERVES 4

PREPARATION + COOKING
10 + 10 minutes + chilling

STORAGE
Leftovers will keep in the refrigerator up to 1 day.

SERVE THIS WITH ...
Cranberry & Almond Quinoa
   (see page 59)
Choco-Nut Ice Cream
   (see page 139)
fresh fruit and plain yogurt

HEALTH BENEFITS
Protein-rich seafood also provides zinc, selenium, and calcium, plus an abundance of essential fats.

1 Mix the olive oil, paprika, tomato paste, lime juice, and honey in a large shallow dish. Add the shrimp, fish, and peppers and mix gently; cover and chill 30 minutes.
2 Preheat the broiler to high. Thread the seafood and peppers onto 8 metal skewers, alternating the ingredients. Grill 5 minutes on each side, or until cooked through.
3 Meanwhile, heat the marinade in a pan 1 to 2 minutes until boiling. Serve the kebabs drizzled with the marinade.

orange-glazed sardines

Adding a few orange segments to the pan creates a delicious sweet-sour glaze children love.

2 tbsp. all-purpose flour
½ tsp. paprika
4 sardines, cleaned
  and scaled
2 tbsp. olive oil
½ tsp. harissa (optional)

juice and grated zest of
  2 oranges
2 tbsp. raisins
1 orange, peeled and sliced
¼ cup pine nuts, toasted
2 tbsp. chopped cilantro leaves

1 Mix the flour and paprika on a plate, then turn the sardines in the mixture to coat them all over; dust off any excess.
2 Mix half the oil with the harissa, if using (it's very hot), the orange juice and zest, raisins, and orange slices.
3 Heat the remaining oil in a skillet and fry the sardines 2 to 3 minutes on each side until brown and crisp. Add the orange slices and their sauce and boil 1 minute, or until slightly thicker.
4 Scatter the pine nuts and cilantro over the sardines and serve immediately.

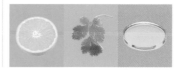

sesame-polenta chicken strips

Try these crisp, baked chicken bites for a delicious and nutritious alternative to battered and deep-fried chicken nuggets.

olive oil, for greasing
¾ cup polenta or cornmeal
¼ cup sesame seeds
2 tbsp. grated Parmesan
  cheese
1 lb. skinless, boneless
  chicken breast halves, cut
  into thin strips

2 eggs, beaten
1 lemon, cut into wedges,
  to serve (optional)

Tomato Dip:
4 tbsp. mayonnaise
2 tbsp. tomato paste or
  sugar-free tomato catsup

1 Preheat the oven to 400°F and grease a baking sheet with oil. To make the dip, mix the mayonnaise and tomato paste in a bowl, then cover with plastic wrap and chill.
2 Mix the polenta, sesame seeds, and Parmesan together in a shallow bowl. Dip the chicken strips in the egg, then coat them in the polenta and put them on the baking sheet. Bake 15 to 20 minutes until golden and crisp.
3 Serve with the tomato dip and lemon wedges, if using.

SERVES 4

PREPARATION + COOKING
10 + 20 minutes

STORAGE
Leftovers will keep in the refrigerator up to 2 days.

SERVE THIS WITH ...
steamed carrots and broccoli couscous
Strawberry Cheesecake
  (see page 128)

HEALTH BENEFITS
Golden polenta, made from cornmeal, is a culinary staple in northern Italy. It is a complex carbohydrate that provides slow-release energy, fiber, and B vitamins.

turkey satay

The satay sauce is a great dip for crudités, too.

SERVES 4

PREPARATION AND COOKING
15 + 10 minutes + chilling

STORAGE
The sauce can be prepared
in advance and chilled until
required. Leftovers will keep in
the refrigerator up to 2 days.

SERVE THIS WITH ...
steamed leafy greens

HEALTH BENEFITS
Turkey is a good source of
protein and provides the amino
acid tryptophan: important for
the production of the brain-
calming chemical serotonin.
Turkey is also rich in selenium,
zinc, and B vitamins.

1 lb. skinless, boneless turkey
    breast, cut into strips
2 tsp. olive oil
1 garlic clove, crushed
2 tbsp. tamari
1 tbsp. peeled and finely grated
    ginger root
zest of 1 lime
2 tbsp. chopped cilantro leaves

Satay Sauce:
1 tbsp. olive oil
2 shallots, finely chopped
1 garlic clove, crushed
2 tsp. peeled and finely grated
    ginger root
¾ cup smooth peanut butter
²/₃ cup coconut milk
1 tbsp. lime juice
2 tbsp. tamari
1 tsp. sweet chili sauce

1 Put the turkey in a dish. Mix the oil, garlic, tamari, ginger,
and lime together, then pour over the turkey. Cover with
plastic wrap and chill 2 hours.

2 For the sauce, heat the oil in a pan and fry the shallots,
garlic, and ginger 2 minutes until soft. Transfer to a food
processor and puree with the remaining ingredients.

3. Preheat the broiler to high. Drain the turkey, reserving
the marinade. Thread the strips onto 12 metal skewers,
brush with the marinade, and broil 5 to 7 minutes until
cooked through, turning once.

4 Heat the sauce until warm. Spoon a little of the sauce
over the skewers, sprinkle with the cilantro, and serve.

Tex-Mex burgers

These burgers are made from lean, protein-rich beef with some extra veggies. They are broiled rather than fried to reduce saturated-fat content.

1 red onion, grated
½ tsp. ground cumin
½ tsp. paprika
14 oz. lean ground beef
1 carrot, grated

2 tsp. Worcestershire sauce
1 egg, beaten
8 wholewheat hamburger buns
2 tomatoes, sliced
handful of mixed salad leaves

1 Mix the onion, cumin, paprika, beef, carrot, and Worcestershire sauce in a large bowl. Add the egg and mix well. Shape the mixture into 8 small burgers. Put them on a plate, cover, and chill 30 minutes.
2 Preheat the broiler to high. Put the burgers on a baking sheet and broil 4 minutes on each side, or until they are cooked through.
3 Cut the buns in half and toast lightly. Fill each one with 1 burger and sliced tomato and salad leaves and serve.

MAKES 8

PREPARATION + COOKING
10 + 8 minutes + chilling

STORAGE
Leftovers will keep in the refrigerator up to 1 day.

SERVE THIS WITH ...
potato salad
Hazelnut-Cherry Tart
  (see page 130)

HEALTH BENEFITS
Beef is an energizer for the brain because it is rich in protein and contains plenty of iron, zinc, and certain B vitamins.

beef tortillas with balsamic onions

Soft, warm tortillas are fabulous filled with tangy onions and strips of lean beef.

SERVES 4

PREPARATION + COOKING
10 + 25 minutes

STORAGE
Leftovers will keep in the refrigerator up to 1 day.

SERVE THIS WITH ...
diced cucumber in a minty yogurt dressing
Apricot & Orange Soufflés (see page 125)

HEALTH BENEFITS
Although wine might not be the first ingredient that springs to mind for a child's meal, red wine contains important antioxidant benefits, and here the alcohol evaporates during cooking.

2 tbsp. olive oil
2 red onions, thinly sliced
1 tbsp. soft brown sugar
3 tbsp. balsamic vinegar
6 tbsp. red wine (optional)

12 oz. cold roast beef, thinly sliced
4 wholewheat flour tortillas
handful of baby spinach leaves
freshly ground black pepper

1 Heat the oil in a saucepan. Add the onions and cook slowly 10 to 15 minutes until they caramelize.
2 Add the sugar, vinegar, and wine and cook 10 minutes longer, stirring occasionally. Set aside and leave to cool, then season with black pepper.
3 Arrange the beef on the tortillas and top with the spinach leaves and then with the balsamic onions. Fold over the sides and roll up the tortillas. Slice in half diagonally and serve.

salmon fishcakes

These fishcakes use antioxidant-rich sweet potato for extra health benefits.

1 large sweet potato, about
   10 oz.
10 oz. salmon fillet
2 tbsp. lemon juice
1 tbsp. chopped dill
grated zest of 1 lemon
1 egg, beaten
1 cup wholewheat bread
   crumbs
2 tsp. olive oil

freshly ground black pepper

Sun-Dried Tomato Mayo:
6 tbsp. mayonnaise
1 tsp. lemon juice
1 tsp. sun-dried tomato paste
3 sun-dried tomatoes in oil,
   drained and finely chopped

1 Preheat the oven to 400°F. Wrap the potatoes in foil and bake 1 hour, or until soft. When cool, peel and mash. Mix all the mayo ingredients together, cover, and chill.

2 Put the salmon in a baking dish with the lemon juice. Cover and bake 20 minutes, or until the flesh is opaque and flakes easily. Cool, then discard the skin and flake the fish.

3 Mix the salmon, dill, and lemon zest into the potatoes. Season with black pepper, cover, and chill 30 minutes.

4 Shape into small patties, then coat in the beaten egg and bread crumbs. Put on a baking sheet and chill 30 minutes.

5 Drizzle the olive oil over the fishcakes and bake 20 to 30 minutes until crisp and golden. Serve with the tomato mayo.

MAKES 10 TO 12

PREPARATION + COOKING
20 minutes + 1 hour 45 minutes
+ chilling

STORAGE
Leftovers will keep in the refrigerator up to 2 days. Freeze uncooked up to 1 month and defrost in the refrigerator before cooking.

SERVE THIS WITH ...
steamed leafy greens
Strawberry Cheesecake
  (see page 128)

HEALTH BENEFITS
Salmon is one of the healthiest brain foods because it is rich in protein and provides one of the best sources of the omega-3 fatty acids OHA and EPA.

teriyaki salmon

This Japanese-inspired marinade is perfect for
oily fish, such as salmon or mackerel, and just
as good with lean meat or poultry, too.

2 tbsp. olive oil
½-inch piece ginger root,
  peeled and grated
1 garlic clove, crushed
juice and grated zest of 1 lime
4 tbsp. tamari
2 tbsp. honey
3 tbsp. mirin (Japanese sweet
  rice wine)
12 oz. skinless, boneless
  salmon fillet, cut into
  thick strips

3 scallions, finely sliced
8 oz. mixed stir-fry vegetables,
  such as bean sprouts, bell
  peppers, bok choy, and
  snow peas
2 tsp. sesame oil
handful of cilantro
  leaves, chopped
1 tbsp. sesame seeds

1 Heat half the oil in a small pan and fry the ginger and
garlic 1 minute. Add the lime juice, zest, tamari, honey,
and mirin. Cook 1 minute until thick and syrupy. Set this
sauce aside.

2 Heat the remaining oil in a nonstick skillet or wok and fry
the salmon 1 to 2 minutes. Add the scallions and stir-fry
the vegetables with a splash of water. Cover and cook
1 to 2 minutes until the vegetables are soft.

3 Pour in the sauce, sesame oil, cilantro, and sesame
seeds and heat through. Serve immediately.

pasta with smoked trout & broccoli

This satisfying dish is ideal when time is limited and everyone's hungry.

14 oz. pappardelle
  or tagliatelle
1 tbsp. olive oil
1 garlic clove, crushed
2 shallots, finely chopped
7 oz. sprouting broccoli
  or 1½ cups broccoli florets
juice and grated zest of 1 lemon

4 tbsp. crème fraîche
2 tbsp. chopped basil leaves
2 tbsp. pine nuts
1 lb. smoked trout, skinned and
  flaked into large chunks
2 tbsp. grated Parmesan
  cheese

1 Cook the pasta in boiling water according to the package directions, about 12 minutes, until *al dente*.
2 Meanwhile, heat the oil in a skillet and cook the garlic and shallots, stirring, 2 minutes. Add the broccoli and lemon juice and zest and cook 3 to 4 minutes longer.
3 Stir in the crème fraîche, basil, and pine nuts and heat through for a few seconds.
4 Drain the pasta well, then add it and the trout to the broccoli mixture. Mix well, sprinkle with the Parmesan, and serve.

SERVES 4

PREPARATION + COOKING
10 + 12 minutes

STORAGE
Leftovers will keep in the refrigerator up to 1 day.

SERVE THIS WITH ...
green salad
Fruit Layer Crisp (see page 134)

HEALTH BENEFITS
Salmon and trout are oily fish, rich in omega-3 fatty acids. Trout is also a good source of niacin, and vitamins B12 and B5, which are important B vitamins for the production of energy and neurotransmitters. Broccoli is packed with antioxidants that help to support the immune system.

690

Mediterranean fish packages

HEALTH BENEFITS
Halibut is a valuable protein food that's packed with a variety of nutrients, including selenium, magnesium, B-group vitamins B12, B6, and niacin, and (perhaps most important) the beneficial omega-3 essential fatty acids.

Baking fish in little paper packages keeps it wonderfully moist and flavorful. The combination of protein, essential fats, and other nutrients makes for a powerful brain-boosting meal. Assemble this dish in advance and chill it until you are ready to cook.

juice and zest of 1 lemon
1 bottled roasted red bell
   pepper in oil, drained
3 tbsp. olive oil
1 tsp. sun-dried tomato paste
4 halibut fillets, about
   4 oz. each

8 pitted black olives, halved
1 tbsp. capers, rinsed
8 cherry tomatoes, quartered
8 basil leaves

SERVES 4

PREPARATION + COOKING
15 + 25 minutes

STORAGE
Leftovers will keep in the
refrigerator up to 1 day.

1 Preheat the oven to 350°F. Cut squares of baking parchment paper and foil, each large enough to wrap up a portion of fish. Put a piece of parchment on top of each piece of foil.

2 Put the lemon juice, zest, red pepper, olive oil, and sun-dried tomato paste in a blender and blend to make a thick paste.

3 Put 1 halibut fillet in the middle of each foil-and-parchment square. Scatter the olives, capers, tomatoes, and basil leaves over and top with the pepper paste. Wrap up the parchment to enclose the fish, folding the edges together to seal the packages, then put on a baking sheet.

4 Bake 25 minutes. Transfer the packages to plates, serve, and unwrap carefully at the table.

SERVE THIS WITH ...
steamed spinach
brown rice
Cranberry & Almond Quinoa
   (see page 59)
Hazelnut-Cherry Tart
   (see page 130)

The essential oil
in basil is a tonic
for the nervous
system and helps
to lift mental
fatigue.

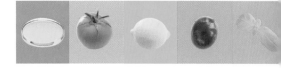

070

😋 😋 😋 😋 😋

creamy fish pie

An all-in-one meal, this family-style dish is rich in antioxidants and packed with flavor.

SERVES 4 TO 6

PREPARATION + COOKING
20 + 55 minutes

STORAGE
Assemble and chill the pie up to 1 day in advance of cooking. If the shrimp have not been frozen, the uncooked pie can be frozen 1 month. Defrost in the refrigerator before cooking. Cooked leftovers will keep in the refrigerator up to 1 day.

SERVE THIS WITH ...
steamed green beans
Fruit Gels (see page 136)

HEALTH BENEFITS
Besides being an excellent source of protein, white fish also contains plenty of B vitamins, particularly B12 and B6, both of which are needed to keep homocysteine levels low. High levels of homocysteine can damage blood vessels and impair brain function.

3 large sweet potatoes, about 1 lb. 10 oz., peeled and cut into chunks
1 tbsp. olive oil
1 garlic clove, crushed
6 oz. skinless salmon fillet
4 oz. each skinless smoked haddock fillet and skinless firm white fish fillet
2 tbsp. lemon juice

2 cups crème fraîche
2 tbsp. chopped parsley
¾ cup grated cheddar cheese
5 oz. shelled cooked shrimp, defrosted if frozen
²/₃ cup frozen peas
²/₃ cup canned corn kernels, drained
2 hard-boiled eggs, quartered

1 Preheat the oven to 375°F. Boil the sweet potatoes for 15 minutes, or until tender, then drain.

2 Meanwhile, heat the oil in a large skillet. Fry the garlic and fish 4 to 5 minutes, then add the lemon juice. Transfer the fish to a baking dish, breaking it into large chunks.

3 Add the crème fraîche, parsley, and half the cheese to the skillet and simmer 2 minutes. Stir in the shrimp, peas, and corn.

4 Mash the sweet potatoes with 1 tbsp. of the sauce. Pour the shrimp mixture over the fish and mix gently. Top with the potato and eggs. Sprinkle with the remaining cheese. Bake 30 to 40 minutes until golden, then serve.

sesame-lemon turkey

This delicious stir-fry is a great introduction to healthy, homemade Chinese food.

2 tbsp. lemon juice
grated zest of 1 lemon
1 tbsp. honey
1 tsp. sesame oil
3 tbsp. tamari
1 lb. skinless, boneless turkey
    breast, cut into strips
2 tbsp. sesame seeds
1 tbsp. olive oil

2 shallots, finely chopped
4 oz. snow peas, trimmed
2 small bok choy,
    leaves separated
1½ cups sliced shiitake
    mushrooms
4 scallions, sliced
2 tbsp. chopped cilantro leaves

1 Mix the lemon juice, zest, honey, sesame oil, and 2 tbsp. of the tamari in a bowl. Add the turkey and mix well, then cover and chill 30 minutes.
2 Lightly toast the sesame seeds until golden brown in a large dry skillet or wok, shaking often. Remove from the pan and set aside.
3 Add the olive oil and shallots to the pan and fry until soft. Add the turkey and marinade and continue cooking 5 to 7 minutes, tossing gently, until golden brown.
4 Add the snow peas, bok choy, mushrooms, and scallions. Stir-fry 1 to 2 minutes until the bok choy begins to wilt. Stir in the sesame seeds and remaining tamari. Sir-fry 1 to 2 minutes longer, sprinkle with cilantro, and serve.

SERVES 4

PREPARATION + COOKING
10 + 15 minutes + chilling

STORAGE
Leftovers will keep in the refrigerator up to 2 days

SERVE THIS WITH …
rice noodles
Pineapple & Mint Frozen Yogurt
  (see page 138)

HEALTH BENEFITS
Leafy greens such as bok choy, spinach, and kale are all a great source of B vitamins, including folate, which aids cognitive ability.

072

turkey meatballs in five-veg sauce

These meatballs are simply irresistible.

SERVES 4–6

PREPARATION + COOKING
20 minutes + 1 hour

STORAGE
Leftovers will keep in the
refrigerator up to 2 days.

SERVE THIS WITH ...
wholewheat spaghetti
Pear, Blackberry & Walnut
  Crumble (see page 127)

HEALTH BENEFITS
Antioxidant-rich carrots also
contain vitamin K, which
is known to enhance
cognitive function and
improve brainpower.

1 red onion, grated
1 garlic clove, crushed
1 lb. ground turkey
1 egg, beaten
¾ cup bread crumbs
1 tbsp. olive oil

Five-Veg Sauce:
1 tbsp. olive oil

2 shallots, chopped
1 garlic clove, crushed
1 celery stick, chopped
1 carrot, chopped
1 red bell pepper, chopped
1 can (15-oz.) tomatoes
1 tbsp. tomato paste
1 tbsp. balsamic vinegar
3 tbsp. apple juice

1 Mix together the onion, garlic, turkey, and egg, then stir
in the bread crumbs. Shape the mixture into 16 small balls.
2 Heat the oil in a skillet and fry the meatballs 5 minutes,
or until golden; transfer to a baking dish.
3 Heat the oil for the sauce in a saucepan. Fry the shallots
and garlic 2 minutes. Add the celery, carrot, and pepper
and cook 1 to 2 minutes. Stir in the remaining ingredients.
Bring to a boil, then reduce the heat and simmer, covered,
15 minutes.
4 Preheat the oven to 350°F. Puree the sauce and pour
it over the meatballs. Cover with foil and bake 30 minutes,
or until cooked through, then serve.

five-spice duck

Children will adore the Asian-style combination of duck with sweet orange syrup.

4 boneless duck breasts, about
   4 oz. each, skin on
1 tsp. Chinese five-spice
   powder
2 tbsp. olive oil

2 star anise, crushed
4 scallions, chopped
2 tsp. honey or agave nectar
1 tbsp. tamari
3 tbsp. orange juice

1 Preheat the oven to 375°F. Cut a few slashes into each duck breast. Rub with the five-spice powder, put in a dish, and drizzle with half the oil.
2 Heat a skillet. Add the duck breasts, skin-side down, and brown the skin, then reduce the heat slightly and cook 5 minutes.
3 Heat a roasting pan in the oven. Put the duck in the pan. Add the star anise, scallions, honey, tamari, and orange juice. Roast 10 minutes, or until the duck is cooked through.
4 Remove from the oven and leave to rest 5 minutes. Slice thinly and serve topped with the onions and sauce.

SERVES 4

PREPARATION + COOKING
15 + 17 minutes

STORAGE
Leftovers will keep in the refrigerator up to 2 days.

SERVE THIS WITH ...
rice noodles
mixed salad
Mango & Orange Fool
  (see page 132)

HEALTH BENEFITS
Duck is rich in protein, iron, B vitamins, and selenium: nutrients that aid memory, concentration, and learning.

Caribbean chicken

Children always find colorful dishes tempting.

4 tbsp. all-purpose flour
8 chicken thighs
1 tbsp. olive oil
½ tsp. saffron strands
½ tsp. turmeric
½ Scotch bonnet chili, seeded
    and finely chopped
2 garlic cloves, crushed
2 scallions, chopped
4 tomatoes, quartered
scant 1 cup coconut milk
juice and grated zest of 1 lime
1 red bell pepper, seeded and
    diced
1 yellow bell pepper, seeded
    and diced
1 mango, peeled, pitted,
    and chopped
freshly ground black pepper

1 Preheat the oven to 400°F. Put the flour in a dish and season with black pepper. Turn the chicken thighs in the flour until evenly coated.

2 Heat the oil in a flameproof casserole and brown the chicken on both sides 2 to 3 minutes; remove from the pan. Add the saffron, turmeric, chili, garlic, and scallions and stir 1 minute. Stir in the tomatoes, coconut milk, lime juice, zest, peppers, and mango.

3 Add the chicken, cover, and bake 15 minutes, then uncover and continue baking 30 to 35 minutes longer, or until the chicken is golden and cooked through—the juices will run clear when the thickest part of the chicken is pierced with a skewer. Serve hot.

sweet & sour chicken

Forget sugary, store-bought sauces and make this delicious recipe using fresh ingredients.

2 tbsp. olive oil

14 oz. skinless, boneless chicken breast halves, cut into chunks

8 oz. mixed stir-fry vegetables, such as carrots, bell peppers, mushrooms, and snow peas

¾ cup drained canned pineapple pieces

3 tbsp. dry-roasted peanuts

Sweet & Sour Sauce:

2 tomatoes

1 carrot

1 shallot

¼ cup dates

3 sun-dried tomatoes in oil, drained

2 tbsp. rice wine vinegar

2 tbsp. tamari

1 garlic clove

1 tbsp. tomato paste

½ cup pineapple juice

1 Puree all the sauce ingredients in a food processor or blender until smooth, then set aside.

2 Heat a wok and add the olive oil. Stir-fry the chicken 3 to 4 minutes until golden brown.

3 Add the vegetables, pineapple, and sauce and continue stir-frying 2 to 3 minutes until the vegetables are cooked but still crisp and the chicken is cooked through.

4 Sprinkle the peanuts over and serve.

SERVES 4

PREPARATION + COOKING
15 + 7 minutes

STORAGE
Leftovers will keep in the refrigerator up to 2 days. The sauce can be prepared in advance and kept in the refrigerator up to 3 days or in the freezer up to 1 month. Defrost in the refrigerator before using.

SERVE THIS WITH ...
brown basmati rice
Tropical Crème Brûlée
  (see page 135)

HEALTH BENEFITS
Pineapple contains bromelain, a compound that can aid protein digestion and reduce inflammation, keeping brains fueled and healthy. It also provides plenty of vitamin C and manganese, which are important for antioxidant protection throughout the body.

SERVES 4

PREPARATION + COOKING
5 + 22 minutes

STORAGE
Leftovers will keep in the
refrigerator up to 2 days

SERVE THIS WITH...
mashed sweet potatoes
steamed vegetables
Fruit Gels (see page 136)

HEALTH BENEFITS
Canned tomatoes are an
excellent source of antioxidants,
including lycopene.

bean & sausage hotpot

Guaranteed to satisfy every hungry child, this
hearty dish is super healthy when made with
high-quality link sausages and mixed beans.

2 tsp. olive oil
8 good-quality link sausages
2 garlic cloves, crushed
2 thyme sprigs
2 red bell peppers, seeded
    and sliced

2 cans (15-oz.) canned mixed
    beans, drained and rinsed
2 cans (15-oz.) crushed
    tomatoes
freshly ground black pepper

1 Heat the oil in a large flameproof casserole. Add
the sausages, garlic, thyme, and peppers and fry
3 to 4 minutes, turning occasionally, until golden brown.
2 Add the beans and tomatoes and bring to a simmer,
then cover and leave to simmer 15 minutes, or until the
sausages are cooked through and the sauce thickens.
3 Season with black pepper and then serve.

pork with apples & pears

The sweet, roasted fruit and creamy sauce that go with this pork dish are perfect for children.

2 tbsp. olive oil
1 tbsp. butter
3 apples, peeled, cored, and quartered
2 pears, peeled and quartered
²/₃ cup apple juice
1 cinnamon stick, broken in half

pinch of apple pie spice
4 pieces lean pork tenderloin, about 4 oz. each
1 tbsp. rosemary leaves
3 tbsp. crème fraîche
freshly ground black pepper

SERVES 4

PREPARATION + COOKING
10 + 30 minutes

STORAGE
Leftovers will keep in the refrigerator up to 2 days.

SERVE THIS WITH ...
corn on the cob
steamed new potatoes and curly kale
Hazelnut-Cherry Tart (see page 130)

HEALTH BENEFITS
Apples contain plant compounds called phenolics, which help to protect the brain from free-radical damage. They are also rich in soluble fiber to help regulate blood-sugar levels and are a good source of boron, which can aid mental alertness and concentration.

1 Preheat the oven to 400°F. Heat a small roasting pan, add half the oil and the butter, and swirl until the butter melts. Add the fruit, apple juice, cinnamon, and apple pie spice. Turn to coat the fruit in the liquid. Bake 20 to 25 minutes until tender and light brown.

2 Meanwhile, preheat the broiler to high. Rub the remaining oil over the pork tenderloins, put on the broiler pan, and sprinkle with pepper and rosemary. Broil 15 minutes, or until cooked through, turning once; leave to rest 5 minutes.

3 Stir the crème fraîche into the fruit and simmer 1 to 2 minutes until slightly thicker. Arrange the fruit with the pork, spoon the sauce over, and serve.

Vietnamese pork

Children will adore the flavors and textures of this sweet and sticky noodle salad with crispy duck.

SERVES 4

PREPARATION + COOKING
15 + 10 minutes + marinating

STORAGE
Leftovers will keep in the refrigerator up to 1 day

SERVE THIS WITH ...
cucumber and mint salad
Tropical Crème Brûlée
(see page 135)

HEALTH BENEFITS
Pork is naturally low in fat and an excellent source of protein. It is also rich in B vitamins.

2 tbsp. fish sauce
1 lemongrass stalk,
    finely chopped
1 garlic clove, crushed
1 tbsp. honey or agave nectar
1 tbsp. sesame oil
14 oz. pork tenderloin,
    cut into strips
1 tbsp. olive oil
6 oz. rice noodles
½ cucumber, peeled and cut
    into strips

2 carrots, cut into strips
1 red bell pepper, seeded and
    cut into thin strips
3 tbsp. chopped mint, chopped
¼ cup roasted cashew nuts

Dressing:
2 tbsp. tamari
1 tbsp. balsamic vinegar
1 tsp. sesame oil
2 tsp. omega oil or flax-seed oil

1 Mix together the fish sauce, lemongrass, garlic, honey and sesame oil in a dish. Add the pork, mix well, then cover and marinate in the refrigerator 30 minutes.

2 Heat the olive oil in a wok and stir-fry the pork 5 to 6 minutes until golden brown and cooked through.

3 Cook the noodles according to the package directions, then drain and rinse. Toss in the cucumber, carrots, red pepper, and mint.

4 Mix the dressing ingredients together and toss with the salad. Serve topped with the pork and cashew nuts.

glazed lamb

Great for jazzing up meat dishes, sweet pomegranate molasses is available in large supermarkets and Middle Eastern groceries.

1 tbsp. tamari
1 garlic clove, crushed
5 tbsp. pomegranate molasses
4 pieces lamb tenderloin, about
    4 oz. each

2 tsp. olive oil
2 tbsp. lemon juice
1 tbsp. honey

1 Mix together the tamari, garlic, and 3 tbsp. of the molasses. Pour over the lamb tenderloins, cover, and marinate in the refrigerator 1 hour or overnight.
2 Preheat the broiler to high. Put the lamb on the broiler pan, reserving the marinade. Broil 15 minutes, turning halfway through, or until cooked through. Leave to rest 5 minutes, then cut into thin slices.
3 Put the marinade, oil, lemon juice, honey, and remaining molasses in a pan. Simmer 1 to 2 minutes until syrupy and serve with the lamb.

SERVES 4

PREPARATION + COOKING
10 + 17 minutes + marinating

STORAGE
Leftovers will keep in the refrigerator up to 2 days.

SERVE THIS WITH ...
steamed leafy green vegetables
mashed sweet potatoes
Fruity Phyllo Packages
  (see page 126)

HEALTH BENEFITS
Lamb is an excellent source of protein, a good source of iron and vitamin B12 to support the production of red blood cells and prevent anemia, and contains zinc, which is vital for brain function.

080

Moroccan lamb

PREPARATION + COOKING
15 minutes + 1 hour 8 minutes

STORAGE
Leftovers will keep in the refrigerator up to 2 days.

SERVE THIS WITH ...
couscous
Fruit Layer Crisp
(see page 134)

HEALTH BENEFITS
One of the top sources of vitamin C and beta-carotene, red bell peppers are useful for reducing inflammation and supporting our immune health—great for keeping our children active and healthy over the winter months.

The savory lamb combined with sweet fruit appeals to palates of all ages.

1 tbsp. olive oil
14 oz. lean boneless lamb, cut into chunks
1 tsp. each ground coriander, ginger, cinnamon, and paprika
1 onion, finely chopped
2 garlic cloves, crushed
juice and grated zest of 1 lemon

1 tbsp. honey or agave nectar
1 red bell pepper, seeded and cut into chunks
1 sweet potato, peeled and diced
10 cherry tomatoes
1¾ cups chicken stock
16 dried apricots
2 tbsp. slivered almonds, lightly toasted

1 Preheat the oven to 375°F. Heat the oil in a large flameproof casserole. Fry the lamb with the spices, onion, and garlic 3 to 4 minutes until the meat browns.
2 Add the lemon juice, zest, honey, red pepper, sweet potato, tomatoes, and stock. Bring to a boil, then cover, transfer to the oven, and bake 40 minutes.
3 Add the apricots and cook 20 minutes longer until the lamb is very tender. Serve sprinkled with the almonds.

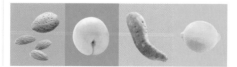

creamy beef korma

Any children who like spicy food will adore this mild curry, which is made with less saturated fat than conventional recipes or carry-outs.

½-in. piece of ginger root, peeled
2 garlic cloves, crushed
1 red onion, chopped
1 tbsp. olive oil
½ tsp. turmeric
1 tsp. ground coriander
1 tsp. garam masala
14 oz. lean beef tenderloin or braising steak, cubed

5 tbsp. finely ground blanched almonds
1 cup lamb or chicken stock
6 tbsp. crème fraîche
3 tomatoes, chopped
handful of slivered almonds, toasted
handful of cilantro leaves, chopped

1 Puree the ginger, garlic, and onion to a paste in a blender.
2 Heat the oil in a large saucepan. Add the paste, turmeric, ground coriander, and garam masala and cook 1 minute, stirring over low heat. Add the beef and cook, stirring, 5 minutes, or until evenly brown.
3 Process the almonds, stock, and crème fraîche in a blender until smooth, then stir this into the beef with the tomatoes. Bring to a boil, reduce the heat, cover, and simmer 20 to 30 minutes until the beef is cooked through.
4 Scatter with the almonds and cilantro and serve.

SERVES 4

PREPARATION + COOKING
15 + 40 minutes

STORAGE
Leftovers will keep in the refrigerator up to 2 days.

SERVE THIS WITH …
brown basmati rice

HEALTH BENEFITS
Creamy commercial curry sauces are often loaded with saturated fat, sugars, and additives, all of which can have a detrimental effect on brain function.

*chow mein

HEALTH BENEFITS
A potent immune supporting food, shiitake mushrooms might also be good for brain health. They are one of the few food sources of vitamin D, a hormonelike vitamin that has been shown to help lift mood and depression.

This Chinese-style version of the Italian favorite of spaghetti with a meat sauce is made with lean ground beef and loaded with lots of antioxidant-rich vegetables. For a fun family meal, encourage children to eat this with chopsticks—an activity that will stimulate their minds as much as their tastebuds.

9 oz. wholewheat
   egg noodles
1 tsp. sesame oil
2 tsp. olive oil
1 lb. lean ground beef
1 tsp. five-spice powder
1 garlic clove, crushed
1 tsp. sweet chili sauce
1 carrot, cut into thin strips
   or julienned

½ cup sliced shiitake or button
   mushrooms
2 oz. snow peas, trimmed
1 red bell pepper, seeded
   and sliced
2 tbsp. oyster sauce
2 tbsp. tamari
1 tbsp. rice wine or dry sherry
2 oz. bean sprouts
1 scallion, chopped

SERVES 4

PREPARATION + COOKING
15 + 20 minutes

STORAGE
Leftovers will keep in the
refrigerator up to 2 days.

SERVE THIS WITH...
Mango & Orange Fool
   (see page 132)

1 Cook the noodles according to the package directions;
drain and refresh under cold water. Put in a bowl and toss
with the sesame oil, then set aside.

2 Heat the olive oil in a wok or large skillet. Add the beef,
five-spice powder, garlic, and sweet chili sauce and stir-
fry 5 minutes, or until the meat is light brown.

3 Add the vegetables and stir-fry 2 minutes longer,
or until they begin to soften.

4 Stir in the oyster sauce, tamari, and rice wine and
simmer 4 to 5 minutes until the meat is cooked through.

5 Add the noodles, bean sprouts, and scallion and stir-fry
1 to 2 minutes until hot. Serve immediately.

The white part
of scallions
contains vitamins
B and C; the green
part contains
vitamin A.

Ⓥ Ⓧ Ⓠ Ⓧ Ⓑ Ⓠ Ⓓ Ⓧ

barley risotto

Barley makes a brilliant, creamy risotto that children simply devour.

SERVES 4

PREPARATION + COOKING
15 minutes + 1 hour 5 minutes

STORAGE
Leftovers will keep in the refrigerator up to 2 days

SERVE THIS WITH ...
tomato, cucumber, and romaine lettuce salad
Apricot & Orange Soufflés (see page 125)

HEALTH BENEFITS
Barley contains plenty of fiber, including beta-glucan, which can help to stabilize blood-sugar levels. It is also rich in the antioxidant selenium.

½ cup pearl barley
½ oz. dried mushrooms
2 tbsp. olive oil
1 onion chopped
2 garlic cloves, crushed
¾ cup brown basmati rice
3 cups hot vegetable stock

1 tbsp. tahini
2 cups sliced mushrooms
2 tbsp. chopped parsley
4 tbsp. grated Parmesan cheese
freshly ground black pepper

1 Cover the barley with water and bring to a boil, then simmer 35 minutes, or until just tender; drain. Soak the dried mushrooms 15 minutes in enough boiling water to cover; drain, reserving the liquid.
2 Heat half the oil in a large pan. Fry the onion and garlic until soft. Add the barley and rice. Mix the stock, mushroom liquid, and tahini and slowly pour into the rice, stirring.
3 Add the drained mushrooms and bring to a boil, then reduce the heat. Simmer, uncovered, 20 to 25 minutes until the rice is tender and most of the stock is absorbed.
4 Meanwhile, heat the remaining oil in a skillet. Fry the mushrooms, stirring, 3 to 4 minutes until brown. Add to the risotto with the parsley, Parmesan, and black pepper to taste, then serve immediately.

Ⓥ ✴ ✴ ✴ ✴ ✴ ✴ ✴

lentil moussaka

This easy vegetarian version of the classic Greek dish will be a hit with the whole family.

3 tbsp. olive oil
1 large eggplant, thickly sliced
1 red onion, chopped
1 garlic clove, chopped
1 cup red lentils, rinsed
2 carrots, chopped
1 can (15-oz.) crushed
   tomatoes

4 tbsp. sun-dried tomato paste
2½ cups vegetable stock
1 cup Greek-style yogurt
2 eggs
4 tbsp. grated Parmesan
   cheese

1 Preheat the broiler to high and line the broiler pan with foil. Use 2 tbsp. of the oil to brush the eggplant slices on both sides. Grill 3 to 4 minutes on each side until golden; set aside.

2 Preheat the oven to 375ºF. Heat the remaining oil in a saucepan. Cook the onion and garlic 2 minutes. Stir in the lentils, carrots, tomatoes, tomato paste, and stock and bring to a boil. Reduce the heat, cover, and simmer 20 minutes, or until the lentils are soft.

3 Spread half the lentils in a baking dish. Top with half the eggplant, then the remaining lentils and a final layer of eggplant. Mix the yogurt, eggs, and half the cheese and spoon over the eggplant. Add the remaining cheese.

4 Bake 30 to 35 minutes, or until golden, then serve.

SERVES 4

PREPARATION + COOKING
20 minutes + 1 hour 10 minutes

STORAGE
Assemble and freeze, uncooked, up to 1 month. Defrost in the refrigerator before cooking. Leftovers will keep in the refrigerator up to 2 days

SERVE THIS WITH ...
Greek salad
Mango & Orange Fool
   (see page 132)

HEALTH BENEFITS
Red lentils are a great vegetarian source of iron and provide zinc and B vitamins. They are also rich in protein and fiber, so can provide steady, slow-burning energy to maintain concentration.

chickpea veggie patties

These lightly spiced patties are a fabulous vegetarian alternative to burgers.

SERVES 4

PREPARATION + COOKING
15 + 20 minutes + chilling

STORAGE
Leftovers will keep in the refrigerator up to 3 days or in the freezer, uncooked, 1 month. Defrost in the refrigerator before cooking.

SERVE THIS WITH …
Cranberry & Almond Quinoa
(see page 59)
Strawberry Cheesecake
(see page 128)

HEALTH BENEFITS
Combining chickpeas with grains, such as the wholewheat rolls or pitas, provides all the eight essential amino acids your child's body needs to produce neurotransmitters.

1 tbsp. olive oil, plus extra
for greasing
1 can (15-oz.) chickpeas,
drained and rinsed
½ red onion, grated
1 carrot, grated
1 garlic clove, crushed
2 tbsp. chopped parsley
1 tsp. ground cumin
1 tsp. ground coriander
1 egg
1½ cups wholewheat
bread crumbs
4 wholewheat rolls or
pita breads
handful of mixed salad leaves

1 Grease a baking sheet with oil. Pulse the chickpeas, onion, carrot, garlic, parsley, cumin, and coriander in a food processor to form a coarse paste. Transfer to a bowl and stir in the egg and bread crumbs.

2 Wet your hands to prevent the mixture from sticking and shape it into 8 patties. Put on the baking sheet, cover, and chill 30 minutes.

3 Preheat the oven to 400°F. Brush the patties with the oil and bake 20 minutes, or until golden brown.

4 Meanwhile, split the rolls or pitas in half and toast or warm them in the oven. Fill the breads with salad and a couple of patties and serve.

tofu noodles

Fried tofu has a tempting, crisp texture that is excellent with stir-fried vegetables.

2 tsp. honey or agave nectar
5 tbsp. tamari
2 garlic cloves, crushed
1 tsp. grated ginger root
9 oz. firm tofu
5 oz. rice noodles

3 tbsp. smooth peanut butter
  (without added sugar)
2 tbsp. olive oil
12 oz. stir-fry vegetables, such
  as broccoli, mushrooms,
  bell peppers, and so on

1 Mix the honey, tamari, garlic, and ginger and pour half into a shallow dish, then add the tofu. Turn the tofu in the sauce to coat, cover, and marinate at least 30 minutes.
2 Put the noodles in a bowl, cover with boiling water, and soak 2 minutes. Drain and rinse under cold water. The noodles should still be crisp.
3 Mix the peanut butter into the remaining tamari mixture with ½ cup boiling water.
4 Drain the tofu and reserve the marinade. Heat a wok, add the oil and cook the tofu in batches 2 to 3 minutes until brown; transfer to a plate.
5 Stir-fry the vegetables 2 minutes. Add the noodles, tofu, sauce, and reserved marinade. Stir-fry 2 to 3 minutes until the vegetables are tender but crisp and the liquid reduces slightly. Serve immediately.

SERVES 4

PREPARATION + COOKING
10 + 12 minutes + marinating

STORAGE
Leftovers will keep in the refrigerator up to 2 days

FOLLOW THIS WITH ...
Choco-Nut Ice Cream
  (see page 139)

HEALTH BENEFITS
Tofu, made from soybeans, is a good source of complete protein. (It contains all eight essential amino acids.) It is also rich in B vitamins, low in saturated fat, and is an important nondairy source of calcium and omega-3 essential fats.

DESSERTS

Most children cannot resist a dessert, and this chapter offers lots of brain-boosting options. From comforting family favorites, such as Peach & Almond Rice Pudding or Pear, Blackberry & Walnut Crumble, to creamy cheesecakes, ice creams, and tarts, all the recipes focus on providing key nutrients to fuel the brain without compromising on taste. There are quick treats, like Mango & Orange Fool or Fruit Layer Crisp, as well as more indulgent delights, such as Chocolate & Orange Mousse. These desserts include exotic flavors, a wide variety of splendid fruit, and whole grains. They might be low in sugar (or sugar-free in some cases), but they are also perfect treats Fruit Gels or Choco-Nut Ice Cream will have the whole family smiling.

087

SERVES 4

PREPARATION + COOKING
5 + 40 minutes

STORAGE
Leftovers will keep in the
refrigerator up to 2 days.

SERVE THIS WITH ...
extra slices of fresh peach
Teriyaki Salmon (see page 100)

HEALTH BENEFITS
Almonds and brown rice provide
plenty of B vitamins, fiber, and
slow-release carbohydrates to
help maintain a steady focus.

peach & almond rice pudding

This wonderfully creamy rice pudding
is the ultimate comfort food.

heaped 1 cup long-grain
   brown rice
4 cups milk
2 tsp. lemon juice
4 tsp. finely ground almonds

2 peaches, peeled, pitted,
   and sliced
handful of slivered almonds,
   toasted

1 Put the rice, milk, and lemon juice in a saucepan. Slowly
bring to a boil, then reduce the heat, cover, and simmer
30 minutes, stirring occasionally, or until the rice is tender
and the milk almost all absorbed.
2 Add the almonds and peaches and cook, stirring,
5 minutes, or until the peaches are soft.
3 Spoon into bowls, sprinkle with the slivered almonds
and serve.

apricot & orange soufflés

Children adore this warming, fruity, and exceptionally light dessert. Dried apricots provide the sweetness in place of sugar.

olive oil, for greasing
1/3 cup dried apricots
2 tbsp. cornstarch
1/2 cup orange juice

grated zest of 1 orange
4 eggs, separated
1/4 tsp. cream of tartar
3 tbsp. sugar

1 Preheat the oven to 375°F and lightly grease four to six ramekins with oil. Put the apricots, cornstarch, orange juice, and zest in a blender and blend until smooth. Pour into a pan and bring slowly to a boil, stirring continuously, 2 to 3 minutes until thick; set aside and leave to cool.

2 Beat the egg yolks into the sauce. In a clean bowl, whisk the egg whites with the cream of tartar until they form soft peaks. Add the sugar and whisk until stiff.

3 Stir a little of the egg white into the sauce, then gently fold in the rest. Spoon the mixture into the ramekins, put them on a baking sheet, and bake 12 to 15 minutes until puffed and pale golden. Serve immediately.

SERVES 4 TO 6

PREPARATION + COOKING
15 + 20 minutes

STORAGE
Best eaten immediately. Make the apricot puree in advance and chill up to 1 day.

SERVE THIS WITH ...
Turkey Noodle Soup
  (see page 43)
plain yogurt

HEALTH BENEFITS
Citrus fruit is a great protector for the brain, providing plenty of vitamin C and phytonutrients.

Ⓥ 🍽 🐟 🥜 🚫

fruity phyllo packages

These delightful little finger-food desserts are irresistible hot or cold—and are a tempting way to encourage children to eat more fruit.

SERVES 4

PREPARATION + COOKING
15 + 12 minutes

STORAGE
Leftovers will keep in the refrigerator up to 1 day.

SERVE THIS WITH ...
crème fraîche
Creamy Salmon & Alfalfa Pitas
(see page 49)

HEALTH BENEFITS
Chopped nuts boost protein intake and are a good source of essential fats. Choose raw, unsalted ones and experiment with different kinds.

6 tbsp. olive oil, plus extra
   for greasing
2 eating apples, peeled,
   cored, and diced
2 tsp. lemon juice
½ tsp. cinnamon

3 tbsp. raisins
4 tbsp. chopped mixed nuts
   (raw, unsalted)
8 sheets of phyllo pastry
   dough, each 8 inches square

1 Preheat the oven to 400°F and grease two baking sheets with oil. Mix the apples, lemon juice, cinnamon, raisins, and nuts in a bowl.

2 Put 1 sheet of phyllo dough on a board and brush with a little of the oil, then cover with another sheet. Put a quarter of the apple mixture lengthwise down the middle of the dough, leaving a small gap at the ends.

3 Fold the two long sides of the dough over, then roll up from one narrow end to enclose the filling. Place the package, seam-side down, on a baking sheet, then repeat with the remaining phyllo and filling.

4 Brush the packages with oil and bake 10 to 12 minutes until golden brown. Serve hot or cold.

pear, blackberry & walnut crumble

An all-time favorite, this treat has a fabulously brain-friendly oat-and-walnut crumble topping.

2 pears, peeled, cored,
   and cut into chunks
2 cups blackberries
grated zest of 1 lemon
1 tbsp. lemon juice

2 tbsp. honey
4 tbsp. apple juice
½ cup walnuts, chopped
2 cups rolled oats
3 tbsp. olive oil

1 Preheat the oven to 350°F. Put the pears and blackberries in a shallow baking dish and sprinkle with the lemon zest and juice. Drizzle the honey and 1 tbsp. of the apple juice over.

2 Mix together the walnuts, oats, oil, and remaining apple juice, then spoon the mixture over the fruit and press down gently.

3 Bake 30 minutes, or until golden brown, then serve.

SERVES 4

PREPARATION + COOKING
10 + 35 minutes

STORAGE
Leftovers will keep in the refrigerator up to 2 days

SERVE THIS WITH ...
plain yogurt
Sesame-Polenta Chicken Strips
  (see page 95)

HEALTH BENEFITS
Pears are a low-GI fruit with plenty of vitamin C. They also contain good amounts of copper, which your child's body needs to produce the antioxidant enzyme superoxide dismutase, which helps to protect cells from damage.

091

Ⓥ ✕ ✕ ✕ ✕

*strawberry cheesecake

HEALTH BENEFITS
Strawberries are rich in vitamin C—in fact, just three or four provide a child's daily portion of this important protective vitamin. They also contain anthocyanins, which are powerful antioxidant substances that help to protect brain cells from damage, and zinc, which boosts mental function.

The crust for this fabulous wheatfree cheesecake is made with nutritious oats and almonds, rather than the more traditional sugary crackers. The wonderfully light, yet creamy filling is full of sweet, juicy strawberries.

6oz. oatcakes
¼ cup finely ground almonds
6 tbsp. butter, melted
5 tbsp. honey
3 eggs, beaten
2 cups low-fat ricotta cheese
2 tbsp. cornstarch

1 cup strawberries

Topping:
½ cup strawberry pure fruit
  spread
1 cup strawberries, sliced

SERVES 6

PREPARATION + COOKING
20 + 55 minutes + chilling

STORAGE
Leftovers will keep in the
refrigerator up to 3 days.

SERVE THIS WITH...
Hong Kong Shrimp
  (see page 61)
Tuna Kebabs with Pineapple
  (see page 64)

1 Preheat the oven to 400°F. Process the oatcakes to fine crumbs in a food processor. In a bowl, mix the crumbs with the almonds. Add the melted butter and 2 tbsp. of the honey and mix thoroughly. Press evenly into an 8-inch round springform pan and bake 10 minutes.

2 Put the eggs, cheese, cornstarch, strawberries, and remaining honey in a food processor and process until smooth. Pour onto the crust and bake 10 minutes, then reduce the heat to 300°F and bake 30 minutes longer. Leave to cool in the pan, and then chill 3 hours. Remove the cheesecake from the pan before topping.

3 For the topping, heat the spread in a pan until runny. Mix in the strawberries, then arrange them on top of the cheesecake. Chill 30 minutes longer before serving.

For a change of
topping, try any
other favorite
berry, such as
raspberries or
blueberries.

Ⓥ ⊘ ⊘ ⊗

hazelnut-cherry tart

This moist fruit tart, almost cakelike in texture, is sure to earn cheers of approval from your children.

SERVES 6–8

PREPARATION + COOKING
15 + 35 minutes

STORAGE
Leftovers will keep in the refrigerator up to 3 days

SERVE THIS WITH ...
Choco-Nut Ice Cream
  (see page 139)
a handful of pitted fresh cherries
Salmon Fishcakes (see page 99)

HEALTH BENEFITS
Not only are hazelnuts a source of high-quality protein and fiber, they also contain a plethora of brain-stimulating nutrients, including vitamin E, B vitamins, iron, zinc, calcium, magnesium, and potassium.

4 tbsp. light olive oil, plus
    extra for greasing
¾ cup hazelnuts
4 tbsp. honey
1 cup self-rising wholewheat
    flour
1 egg, beaten
1 tsp. baking powder
¾ cup Greek-style yogurt
1 cup cherries, pitted and
    halved

1 Preheat the oven to 350°F and grease an 8-inch springform pan with oil.
2 Process the nuts in a food processor until finely ground. With the machine running, add the honey, oil, and flour and process until the mixture resembles bread crumbs.
3 Put half the mixture into the pan and press down evenly with the back of a spoon until firm.
4 Add the egg, baking powder, and yogurt to the remaining nut mixture in the food processor and process to form a thick batter. Gently mix in the cherries and spoon the batter over the crust.
5 Bake 30 to 35 minutes until risen, firm, and golden. Leave to cool in the pan, then cut into slices and serve.

Ⓥ ✗ ✗ Ⓒ ✗ ✗

chocolate & orange mousse

This rich, indulgent dessert is actually low in fat and sugar to help your child stay sharp.

6 oz. dark chocolate
    (75% cocoa solids),
    chopped
12 oz. silken tofu

grated zest and juice of
    2 oranges
grated orange zest, to decorate
grated chocolate, to decorate

1 Melt the chocolate in a bowl over a pan of simmering water, stirring occasionally; leave to cool slightly.
2 Purée the tofu, chocolate and orange zest and juice in a food processor or blender until smooth and creamy.
3 Spoon the mixture into four individual dishes and chill 3 hours, or overnight.
4 Decorate with a little orange zest and grated chocolate, then serve.

SERVES 4

PREPARATION + COOKING
10 + 2 minutes + chilling

STORAGE
Make this up to 1 day ahead and chill in the refrigerator until required. Leftovers will keep in the refrigerator up to 2 days.

SERVE THIS WITH ...
a handful of fresh raspberries
Turkey Meatballs in Five-Veg
    Sauce (see page 106)

HEALTH BENEFITS
Silken tofu has no saturated fat and is high in protein as well as calcium and magnesium, which will help your child to wind down after a busy day.

Ⓥ ⊗ ⊗ ⊗ ⊗ ⊗ ⊗

mango & orange fool

Bursting with tropical flavors, this creamy fruit fool takes just minutes to prepare and is sure to disappear almost as quickly.

SERVES 4

PREPARATION
10 minutes + chilling

STORAGE
Best eaten immediately.

SERVE THIS WITH ...
Lemon Oatmeal Cookies
(see page 77)
Vietnamese Pork
(see page 112)

HEALTH BENEFITS
Yogurt contains the amino acid tyrosine, which your child's body needs for the production of the neurotransmitters dopamine and noradrenaline. Yogurt is also a good source of healthy probiotic bacteria.

1 large mango, peeled, pitted,
   and chopped
juice and grated zest of 1 orange
³/₄ cup plain yogurt

scant ½ cup Greek-style yogurt
1 tsp. flax-seed oil
grated zest of 1 orange,
   to decorate

1 Puree the mango and orange juice, and zest in a food processor or blender until smooth.
2 Add both yogurts and the oil and blend until smooth and creamy.
3 Divide the fool into four glasses and chill until required. Decorate with orange zest and serve.

Ⓥ ⊘ ⊘ ⊘ ⊘ ⊘ ⊘ ⊘

summer berry pudding

Bursting with antioxidants, such as vitamin C, this is an easy, no-cook summer treat.

3 tbsp. apple juice
14 oz. mixed berries,
    such as blackberries,
    raspberries, and
    blueberries, plus extra
    to serve

10 to 12 slices wholewheat
    bread, crusts removed

SERVES 4

PREPARATION + COOKING
20 + 5 minutes + chilling

STORAGE
Make up to 1 day in advance
and chill in the refrigerator up
to 2 days.

SERVE THIS WITH...
crème fraîche
Pasta with Smoked Trout
    & Broccoli (see page 101)

HEALTH BENEFITS
Berry fruits provide plenty of
fiber and have a low GI score
compared with many other
fruits. They are also full of highly
active antioxidant and anti-
inflammatory ingredients.

1 Put the apple juice and berries in a pan. Bring to a slow simmer and cook 2 to 3 minutes, or until the juices begin to run from the fruit.

2 From the slices of bread, cut 8 circles large enough to fit the bottom and top of individual pudding molds or ramekins. Cut the remaining bread slices in half. Flatten the pieces of bread with a rolling pin.

3 Line the bottom and side of each mold with half the circles and the strips of bread. Spoon the berries into each mold and top with the remaining bread circles.

4 Fit a saucer on top of each mold and place a weight on the saucer. Stand the puddings on a tray and chill 12 hours, or overnight.

5 Run a knife around the inside edge of each mold and turn the desserts out onto serving plates. Serve with extra berries alongside.

Ⓥ ⊗ Ⓞ ◎ ⊗

fruit layer crisp

This irresistible, antioxidant-packed dessert
will tempt your children with its natural
sweetness, nutty crunch, and vibrant colors.

2 tbsp. olive oil
¾ cup rolled oats
½ cup chopped hazelnuts
½ cup slivered almonds
1 tbsp. honey
1 tbsp. ground flax seeds

3 tbsp. wheat germ
heaped 1 cup blueberries
1 cup raspberries
¾ cup strawberries, hulled
    and sliced
1¼ cups plain yogurt

1 Heat a nonstick skillet and add the oil. Add the rolled
oats and stir to coat in the oil, then cook, stirring,
3 to 4 minutes until golden brown.

2 Add the hazelnuts and almonds and cook, stirring
continuously, 2 to 3 minutes longer until the nuts are
golden. Pour the mixture into a bowl and stir in the honey,
flax seeds, and wheat germ.

3 Mix the blueberries, raspberries, and strawberries
together in a bowl. Divide half the fruit into four glasses
or bowls. Top with half the yogurt, then add a layer
of oat mixture. Repeat, finishing with another
layer of the oat mixture, and serve.

Ⓥ ⊗ ⊗ ⊗ ⊗ ⊗

tropical crème brûlée

This fruity, nutritious dessert will help your children to stay alert—without causing big energy swings.

½ papaya, peeled, seeded, and
  chopped
1 banana, sliced
2 tbsp. orange juice
1¼ cups plain yogurt

2 tbsp. shredded coconut
4 egg yolks
1 tbsp. cornstarch
4 tsp. brown sugar

1 Preheat the oven to 350°F. Mix together the papaya, banana, and orange juice, then divide the mixture into four ramekins.

2 Puree the yogurt, coconut, egg yolks, and cornstarch in a food processor or blender until smooth and spoon the mixture over the fruit.

3 Put the ramekins in a roasting pan and pour in enough hot water to come halfway up the sides. Bake 30 minutes, or until lightly set. Leave to cool, then chill 4 to 5 hours, or overnight.

4 Sprinkle the sugar over the custards and use a blowtorch to caramelize it. Alternatively, preheat the broiler to high and caramelize the sugar under the broiler. Leave to cool before serving.

SERVES 4

PREPARATION + COOKING
15 + 35 minutes + chilling

STORAGE
Make in advance and chill, but do not add the sugar until just before broiling. This will keep in the refrigerator up to 1 day.

SERVE THIS WITH ...
fresh berries
Sesame-Lemon Turkey
  (see page 105)

HEALTH BENEFITS
Papaya contains the enzyme papain, which aids digestion. It is also rich in B vitamins. Banana provides a steady energy release and is a good source of zinc.

*fruit gels

HEALTH BENEFITS
Raspberries are rich in antioxidants and flavonoids that help to protect the body's tissue and cells. They also contain a variety of B vitamins, including folic acid and niacin, which are important for neurotransmitter production.

Colorful red and orange gel layered in a glass makes a perfect party treat. These vibrant gels are a wonderful way to encourage children to eat more fruit. Using fresh juice and whole fruit avoids the need to add sugar.

Red Layer:
1 cup apple juice
2 tbsp. agar agar flakes
2 cups fresh or
    frozen raspberries

Orange Layer:
1 cup orange juice
2 tbsp. agar agar flakes
1¼ cups canned mandarin
    orange segments in natural
    juice, drained
4 tbsp. plain yogurt (optional)

SERVES 4

PREPARATION + COOKING
10 + 5 minutes + chilling

STORAGE
Prepare the jellies up to 1 day
in advance and chill. Leftovers
will keep in the refrigerator
up to 2 days.

SERVE THIS WITH...
Shrimp & Mango Tarts
  (see page 60)
Tex-Mex Burgers (see page 97)

1 Pour the apple juice into a pan and bring to a boil. Add
the agar agar and raspberries and simmer, stirring,
2 minutes, or until the agar agar dissolves.
2 Transfer the mixture to a food processor and process
until smooth. Pass through a strainer, then cool slightly
and divide into four tall glasses. Chill 1 to 2 hours until set.
3 Pour the orange juice into a pan and bring to a boil. Add
the agar agar and mandarin orange slices and simmer,
stirring, 2 minutes, or until the agar agar dissolves.
Transfer the mixture to a food processor and process until
smooth. Pass through a strainer, then cool slightly and
pour over the red layer. Chill 1 to 2 hours until set.
4 Top each jelly with some yogurt, if using, and serve.

Agar agar is
a vegetarian
alternative
to gelatin and
is used here to set
these fruity gels.

660

Ⓥ ⊗ ⊗ Ⓞ ⊗ ⊗ ⊗

pineapple & mint frozen yogurt

Fresh mint gives this easy, fantastic dessert a refreshing lift.

SERVES 4

PREPARATION + FREEZING
10 minutes + 4 hours

STORAGE
Freeze up to 3 months.
Place in the refrigerator
30 minutes before serving.

SERVE THIS WITH ...
fresh chopped pineapple,
mango, and papaya
Lemon Oatmeal Cookies
  (see page 77)
Bean & Sausage Hotpot
  (see page 110)

HEALTH BENEFITS
This dessert is fabulous for
digestive health. The healthy,
probiotic bacteria in yogurt
help to maintain the health
of your child's gut, while the
bromelain in pineapple aids
protein digestion.

2 cups pineapple cubes	**1 tsp. lime juice**
²/₃ cup plain yogurt	**2 tsp. finely chopped mint**

1 Freeze the pineapple cubes 3 to 4 hours until solid.
2 Blend the frozen pineapple, yogurt, lime juice, and mint in a blender until the mixture forms a thick, creamy "ice cream."
3 Serve immediately or pour into a shallow freezerproof container and freeze until required.

V ⊗ ⊗ ⊗ ⊗

choco-nut ice cream

Using frozen fruit, this indulgent ice cream can be whizzed up in minutes. Try other kinds of nuts according to your child's tastes.

7oz. silken tofu
3 bananas
²/₃ cup soy milk
¾ cup hazelnuts, toasted

2 tbsp. honey or agave nectar
4 oz. dark chocolate
   (75% cocoa solids), melted

1 Cut the tofu and bananas into small pieces and freeze 3 to 4 hours.
2 Put the soy milk and hazelnuts in a food processor or blender and process until smooth and creamy.
3 Add the honey and melted chocolate and process until combined, then add the frozen bananas and tofu and process to form a thick, soft "ice cream."
4 Serve immediately or pour into a freezerproof container and freeze until required.

SERVES 4

PREPARATION + FREEZING
15 minutes + 4 hours

STORAGE
Freeze up to 3 months.
Place in the refrigerator
30 minutes before serving.

SERVE THIS WITH ...
Orange-Glazed Sardines
 (see page 94)

HEALTH BENEFITS
A great source of potassium, bananas can aid nerve-cell function and cell communication. Bananas and are also rich in soluble fiber, which slows down the release of sugars from carbohydrates.

five-day menu plans

wheat- and gluten-free menu plan

Many recipes in this book are suitable for those on wheat- and gluten-free diets, and gluten-free flour mixes can be substituted for regular wheat flour in many of the cakes and cookies. One advantage of these recipes is that they rely on fresh ingredients—not processed sauces and condiments that can contain hidden wheat or gluten grains.

Day 1

Breakfast: Vegetable Röstis with Poached Eggs (see page 34)

Lunch: Tomato & Chickpea Soup (see page 44) with rice cakes

Dinner: Creamy Fish Pie (see page 104)

Day 2

Breakfast: Millet & Apple Cereal (see page 28)

Lunch: Hong Kong Shrimp (see page 61)

Dinner: Sweet & Sour Chicken (see page 109) with rice noodles

DAY 3

Breakfast: Pink Zinc Heaven (see page 23)

Lunch: Fabulous Frittata (see page 48)

Dinner: Turkey Satay (see page 96)

DAY 4

Breakfast: Giant Baked Beans on gluten- & wheat-free bread (see page 38)

Lunch: Mexican Bean Tacos (see page 46)

Dinner: Creamy Beef Korma (see page 115)

DAY 5

Breakfast: Peach & Raspberry Shake (see page 24)

Lunch: Cranberry & Almond Quinoa (see page 59)

Dinner: Seafood Kebabs (see page 93)

vegetarian menu plan

Protein is essential for efficient brain function, so make sure to include a wide range of protein-rich foods every day, including eggs, dairy produce, beans, legumes, nuts, seeds, and whole grains. This menu plan is free from meat, poultry, fish, and foods containing gelatin, which is often used in gels. Read labels to make sure cheeses are vegetarian.

Day 1
Breakfast: Apricot & Tofu Boost
   (see page 22)
Lunch: Fabulous Frittata (see page 48)
Dinner: Barley Risotto (see page 118)

Day 2
Breakfast: Popeye Baked Eggs
   (see page 33)
Lunch: Cranberry & Almond Quinoa
   (see page 59)
Dinner: Tofu Noodles (see page 121)

DAY 3
Breakfast: Zesty Citrus Crêpes
   (see page 36)

Lunch: Mexican Bean Tacos (see page 46)
Dinner: Chickpea Veggie Patties
   (see page 120)

DAY 4
Breakfast: Tropical Yogurt Pots
   (see page 30)
Lunch: Veg & Pesto Panini (see page 45)
Dinner: Lentil Moussaka (see page 119)

DAY 5
Breakfast: Breakfast Bars (see page 32)
Lunch: Baked Stuffed Peppers
   (see page 57)
Dinner: Minted Pea & Cheese Omelet
   (see page 58)

nut-free menu plan

Nut allergies can be severe and life threatening, so this menu plan avoids all nuts and their by-products. Nuts are rich in nutrients for brain health, so make sure a nut-free diet is balanced and includes oily fish and seeds to provide essential fats. Cooking without processed foods means it is easy to avoid using nuts, but always check labels to be sure.

Day 1
Breakfast: Oaty Pancakes with
  Hot-Smoked Salmon (see page 37)
Lunch: Moroccan Turkey Wraps
  (see page 53)
Dinner: Pork with Apples & Pears
  (see page 111)

Day 2
Breakfast: Apricot & Tofu Boost
  (see page 22)
Lunch: Fabulous Frittata (see page 48)
Dinner: Five-Spice Duck (see page 107)

Day 3
Breakfast: Popeye Baked Eggs
  (see page 33)

Lunch: Tomato & Chickpea Soup
  (see page 44)
Dinner: Turkey Meatballs in Five-Veg
  Sauce (see page 106)

Day 4
Breakfast: Zesty Citrus Crêpes
  (see page 36)
Lunch: Chicken Spring Rolls (see page 52)
Dinner: Creamy Fish Pie (see page 104)

Day 5
Breakfast: Vegetable Röstis with Poached
  Eggs (see page 34)
Lunch: Steak Ciabatta with Avocado
  (see page 55)
Dinner: Tex-Mex Burgers (see page 97)

vegan menu plan

This menu follows the principles of a vegan diet and avoids any animal-derived foods, such as meat, poultry, seafood, and ingredients that are by-products of animals, including eggs, dairy produce, and honey. A range of grains, beans, legumes, vegetables, fruits, nuts, and seeds helps provide a balanced diet for brain health.

Day 1
Breakfast: Apricot & Tofu Boost
  (see page 22)
Lunch: Beet Cream Soup
  (see page 42)
Dinner: Chickpea Veggie Patties
  (see page 120), made without egg

Day 2
Breakfast: Brain-Berry Muesli
  (see page 26), served with soy milk
Lunch: Veg & Pesto Panini (see page 45),
  made without Parmesan cheese
Dinner: Barley Risotto (see page 118),
  made without Parmesan

Day 3
Breakfast: Millet & Apple Porridge
  (see page 28), made using soy milk

Lunch: Hummus & Seeded Crackers
  (see page 72), made without Parmesan
Dinner: Baked Stuffed Peppers
  (see page 57), using soy cheese

Day 4
Breakfast: Breakfast Bars (see page 32)
Lunch: Tomato & Chickpea Soup
  (see page 44) with oatcakes
Dinner: Cranberry & Almond Quinoa
  (see page 59)

Day 5
Breakfast: Giant Baked Beans on Toasted
  Rye (see page 38)
Lunch: Mexican Bean Tacos (see page 46)
Dinner: Tofu Noodles (see page 121)

INDEX